The Nuts & Bolts Writer's Manual

by Loma G. Davies

Cassell Publications

This publication is designed to provide accurate and authoritative information with regard to the subject matter covered. It is sold with the understanding that neither the publisher nor the author is engaged in rendering legal, accounting, or other professional service regarding the subject matter covered. If legal advice or other expert assistance is desired, the services of a competent professional person should be sought.

The Nuts & Bolts Writer's Manual

Copyright © 1991 by Loma G. Davies

Cover design by Gary W. Amacher

Production services by D & D Enterprise, Pompano Beach.

First edition.

ISBN: 0-942980-16-6

Printed in the United States of America

CONTENTS

Introduction

This book gives you the skills necessary to realize your dream of becoming a published writer. And, for those of you who are already published, it is the refresher course in basic skills everyone needs from time to time.

You will learn how to choose your topic and narrow it down to a manageable size. You will learn how to determine your audience and how to best meet their needs. You will learn how to present your material in the most effective way possible. You will learn how to locate and incorporate specific details into your writing. You also will learn how to write the first draft, examine it critically, and by rewriting make it the best piece of writing possible.

Necessary Writing Tools

As with any profession, a certain amount of equipment is necessary to become a published writer. You need the tools of the trade. These tools include note pads and pens or pencils for making notes and possibly writing first drafts. Some writers compose best at a typewriter or a computer, others with pen and paper. While I use a computer, I still do most first drafts and editing with pen and paper.

I find I can concentrate better looking at a hard copy than staring at a computer screen.

You will need a dictionary, thesaurus, and some type of grammar reference, although the grammar and style chapters in this book should answer most, if not all, of your grammar questions. You also need a market guide or two. If you basically write for the secular market, you need *Writer's Market.* If you do any amount of inspirational writing, you also need *Christian Writers Market Guide.* Both of these book are published annually. As you can afford it, add an almanac and atlas to your collection of reference books.

A typewriter, word processor, or computer is a must for writing your final copy. If you want to, you can write longhand until you get to the final copy. That version MUST be typed. One advantage of a word processor or computer over a typewriter is that editing is much faster. You can add your changes without having to retype the entire manuscript. Some programs also have spell checking programs and on-line thesauruses available.

In today's hi-tech publishing, some editors want copies of your manuscripts on disk as well as hard copies — especially book-length manuscripts. However, I recently received guidelines from a major women's magazine which state it "prefers articles in IBM compatible disk, WordPerfect." If you plan to buy either a word processor or computer, don't buy the first one you see or your friends recommend. Check around, talk to people who use them. Find out what they like and don't like (which may be more important) about their computer and/or software programs. Find out how much dealer help or computer networking is available in your area. Unless you are a "computer whiz," you will need it.

The final copy that you send to the editor should be typed on 16# or 20# bond paper. You can use cheap paper for all copies except the final one. You also will need long business-size envelopes for queries, and large 9x12 or 10x13 envelopes for mailing manuscripts that are more than three pages long. In addition, you will need return address and mailing labels.

You should have some letterheads printed. While you can start a writing career without them, have them done as soon as you become serious about writing, They should be on white or off-white paper. The only information you need on them is your name, address, and telephone number. Simple but attractive is the byword. And while you're at the printer's, you might order some business cards. You can hand them to people when you talk to them about writing jobs. Also, when you make contacts with editors at writers conferences, you will appear more serious and professional if you hand them cards.

You will, of course, need stamps. A postal scale will save time and the frustration of having to check weights at the post office each time you mail an item weighing more than an ounce. Since you have to enclose a self-addressed, stamped envelope with the correct amount of postage attached with your manuscript, you will save time if you are able to put the postage on it at home.

You need #1 metal paper clips to clip manuscripts you send to editors. Do not staple them. You will, however, need a stapler to keep your papers together. File folders and labels are essential for organizing your research, manuscripts, sample copies, et cetera. Index cards (3x5 are fine) are helpful to keep track of important information. They are easy to sort into specific categories when doing research.

As you collect material, you will need a file cabinet or two or three to store your material. To save money, watch classified ads for used cabinets, or you can buy cardboard file boxes quite reasonably.

A mini tape recorder in your car is very helpful to record ideas you think of as you are driving along. Be careful not to take your hands off the steering wheel or your eyes off the road to record ideas, especially in heavy city traffic.

Build a library of writing reference books. Make a list of books you want and hint to your family that you would like some of them as gifts on special occasions. What you include in your writing library will depend on the type of writing you do. Some books are for nonfiction writers, some for fiction writers, and others can help both.

Broaden Your Horizons

Don't fall into the trap of thinking that the only markets for your writing are magazine and book publishers. Keep in mind that someone has to write everything you see in print, including bumper stickers and business advertisements. Look around your town. In all towns, there are people out there who need your services. Make yourself available for a price. Don't wait for the jobs to come to you; you go to the jobs. Explain what you can do for them. Most people don't like to write. That's hard for writers to believe, but it's true. They will be delighted to have a professional take over the chore for them. Some of my other writing jobs include writing a column for an area weekly, and reporting on and taking pictures of anything of interest in my end of the county. I also am staff writer for the SAKW (State Association of Kansas Watersheds).

As you read this book and get started on your way to becoming a professional writer, don't look at other writers who seem to be more successful and think how lucky they are. Create your own luck by reminding yourself of the words of Thomas Jefferson: "I'm a great believer in luck, and I find the harder I work the more I have of it."

Chapter 1:

This and That

Writers have been described as wordsmiths. We use the same dictionary as everyone else and create writing that no one else can quite duplicate, because no one else has quite our temperament or our life experiences. If fifty writers were assigned the same subject, you would have fifty different articles with fifty different slants. Each one would bring along that special something only he possesses.

As writers, we have an awesome responsibility to tell the truth. Have you ever heard someone make an outrageous statement and when you questioned him about his source he said that he read it somewhere? People believe what they see in black and white, so be careful what you put on that page. Once you become a writer you are an authority.

Successful writers communicate information, ideas, and impressions across the barriers of time and space. We transfer our ideas into the minds of people we may never see and, if our ideas are enduring, we will continue to transfer them long after our deaths.

How to be a Successful Writer

To be a successful writer, you must write. Pretend writers just talk about it. You know the type. They are everywhere and not only pretending to be writers. They are pretending to be craftsmen, doctors, and teachers. They spend their time telling you how good they are and how hard they work. If you watch them for a while, however, you find they are more talk than work. If you are busy doing your job, you don't have time to sit around telling people how busy you are. Don't talk writing. Write.

Making Time to Write

To be a successful writer you must set time aside for writing and faithfully use it for that. I once heard of a man who had a burning desire to write a book but found it very difficult to find a quiet time that did not interfere with the rest of his duties. He solved it by getting up each morning at 3:00 a.m. and writing until 6:00 a.m. When he finished his book, he found he was so accustomed to the schedule that he continued his early morning writing. You may not want or be able to give up three hours of sleep to write. But what about a one hour block of time three or four days a week? Check your biological clock. If you are most alert in the morning, schedule your writing time then. If you are a night owl, schedule it after everyone else is in bed.

If you wait for inspiration to strike, you won't get much done. Writing is ninety-nine percent perspiration and one percent inspiration. And usually the inspiration comes while you are busy perspiring. Writing is like any other job. Sometimes you don't feel like working, but you have to. How would your employer react if you called in to say you didn't feel inspired to go to work? Chances are she would suggest you find the inspiration to begin job hunting.

The part-time writer sometimes has difficulty thinking of writing as a regular job. No matter how little time you are able to devote to it, you have to think of writing as a job. You just happen to be the boss and work at home. You will need more determination to go to your work place and write than to go to a regular job. But if you really want to be successful, you are going to have to, even when you don't feel like it.

Managing Your Writing Time

Most writers work another job, so writing time is very limited. To get the most out of this limited time, organization is imperative. There is more to the writing business than just putting words on paper. Life would be nice if all we had to do was write, but that is not the way the writing world works. We must maintain files, find markets, and send out manuscripts. These are all necessary but time-consuming jobs. However, if we get organized, we will have more time to write.

You must have a quiet, permanent place to write, even if it is a corner of a room. Don't use up precious time and energy to get out supplies and files each time you want to type a page or send out a manuscript.

Marketing takes time. By some estimates, it consumes sixty to eighty percent of a freelance writer's time. You can save precious hours by checking *Writer's Market* and *Christian Writers Market Guide.* They list thousands of markets for your material and give important information about each one listed. Make a list of the markets that interest you most. Then transfer the important information for each onto 3x5 index cards. Information to include on the cards:

- name and address of the publication
- the person to send the manuscript to
- whether a query is required
- the audience
- acceptable manuscript length
- how much they pay
- whether they pay on acceptance or publication
- what rights they accept

Next, organize the cards in alphabetical order and put them in a card file. If you have several categories (such as juvenile, teen, adult, inspirational), separate them by category so you do not have to go through all the cards every time you are looking for a specific type of market. If you highlight the information most important to you — payment on acceptance, desired length, rights accepted, you can see at a glance if it is one of your preferred markets. Cards also are updated easily when you learn of a change of editor or address.

A computer can be a real writing timesaver. However, you may find you spend a lot of time trying to locate the disk where an article or story is stored. Again 3x5 cards can solve the problem. Write each article or story title and disk number on a card and alphabetize by article name. Then you can locate any piece of writing in a matter of seconds.

Note: If you use a computer, you should have at least one set and preferably two sets of backup disks for everything you write. You never know when a disk will go bad or be damaged. If it contains the only copy of your material, you are in deep trouble. I make two sets of backups. One is a home set which gets backed up quite regularly, at least once a week, most of the time. The other set I store away from home just in case. The few extra dollars these backups cost can prove invaluable if your originals ever are lost or damaged.

When you have an article or story polished and ready to mail to editors, make a file folder for it. Keep a copy of the article or story and all correspondence in the folder. Either on the outside or inside front of the folder write where you have sent it and the date sent. This saves the time of going through carbon copies of letters to see where you have submitted it. You won't want to resubmit it to a publication that has already rejected it, unless there has been an editor change and you really think it suits that market.

In addition, a notebook listing dates of submission and where an article or story has been submitted will tell you immediately how long it has been at a particular publisher. A glance through a notebook is quicker than checking each file folder. You will see quickly if the piece has been out long enough for a follow-up letter.

To be sure you are slanting your article or story properly for your targeted market, write to the magazine, state you are a writer, and ask for a sample copy and writers guidelines. (The term editorial guidelines is synonymous with writers guidelines.) Market listings, such as those in *Writer's Market,* usually tell you if there is any charge for these. Frequently, you will need to send a self-addressed stamped envelope. Also ask if a *theme list* is available. A theme list tells what special subjects or themes upcoming issues will focus on. These are usually prepared annually and used by ad salesmen to sell advertising space in the magazine. Guidelines and theme lists can help eliminate the frustration of receiving rejection slips saying "This is good, but we just published something similar."

As you receive the sample copies, make a file folder for each. Put the sample copy and guidelines in the folder. File the folders alphabetically in a special drawer of your file cabinet. Now you can easily and quickly find what each publication wants and what its slant is.

Because tax time has a way of coming around every year, you should keep good, accurate records of receipts and expenses in a notebook or on your computer. Then you won't have to wonder if you have forgotten to report income or claim a deduction. Initially, getting organized takes some extra time, but it will pay dividends many times over in time saved and frustration averted.

Characteristics of Creative People

To be successful, writers must be creative. Someone has suggested that creative people possess characteristics or powers that the general population does not have, or at least, does not use. Creative people develop their powers of observation. While others see, we observe. We note details and file them away for later use. We look for the unusual among the mundane. We constantly use our senses to sample the world around us. We then convey vivid word pictures to our readers so they, too, can share our experiences.

As creative people, we let our imaginations run free. We ask "What if?" and examine the possibilities. We ask, "Why?" and are not satisfied with the obvious answers. We peruse and poke and probe until we are satisfied.

Creative people are curious. We analyze our world and do not accept the surface view of how things are or how they work. We always want to know more. We continually research life through reading and observing. We are active listeners, really listening to what people say, not just waiting for our turn to talk.

Creative people are interested in others. We want to know not just what people do, but why they do it. This is the stuff stories are made of, the why behind the action.

Creative people seek new experiences. We do not stay shut up in our little world and peek out at life from behind a pulled curtain. We get out and live it. Only then can we write about it as it really is, not how we think it is. We do not allow ourselves to stay in a rut. If we find we are getting into one, we deliberately set out to create new experiences. We make life an adventure. We take a different route to work, try a new restaurant for lunch, and read a genre of book we usually don't read.

Creative people do not fear emotions. We experience them. We do not hide from our feelings. We observe and learn from them and record our findings in our journals. We then can transfer real emotions to our fictional characters.

The Writer's Journal

A journal is an important writer's tool, especially for those who write fiction. This is the place to jot down ideas and material you think you may be able to use later. Journal jottings can include bits of conversation; an impression of a person, place, or event; a description of a scene or person, et cetera. Your journal is not a diary. It may include what happened, but it also includes your thoughts and feelings about the event, what you saw, read, or heard and what caused it. You should carry a journal or notebook with you at all times. Also keep paper and pen beside your bed for those inspirations that come in the middle of the night. If you wait until morning to write them down, you will find they have fled with the night.

Suggestions to Increase Creativity

1. *Really listen* to music. Get involved in it. Imagine, see, and feel what the composer is trying to express. Visualize the sunrise, the sunset, the war, the quarrel, et cetera.

2. Explore nature. Spend time alone in the woods, the mountains, or just out in the countryside looking at the infinite variations of God's creativity.

3. Watch people. Go to a mall, a ball game, a park, or an airport and observe the people. An international terminal can yield an infinite collection of fascinating people to watch. Jot descriptions in your journal.

4. Spend time in art galleries, museums, zoos — any place where you can have new experiences and people to watch.

5. Everyone has a favorite author. Read or reread something she has written. Observe and enjoy the imagery and writing style that has made her your favorite. Figure out why you prefer her writing over other authors.

6. In today's hectic world we often don't take time to just sit and think. In fact, when we stop being productive and just sit and think, someone may suggest we should be doing something more worthwhile. We even may feel guilty ourselves because we aren't doing something. In this fast-lane world, we are programmed for action, not thinking. But to be a writer, you *must* be a thinker.

7. Listen to the children. *Really listen.* If yours are grown, go to parks, volunteer at schools, work with them in church or scouts, but get involved and listen. You will learn what they are thinking, feeling, and saying; it has changed over the years. The answers may surprise and even shock you.

8. Read an article or story and think about how you would write it differently.

9. Let your emotions work for you. Jot down your feelings when you are happy, sad, or angry. This makes it easier to transfer similar feelings to your characters.

10. Go to a card shop and read some of the verses. Usually there also is an assortment of posters worth perusing.

11. Look over your idea file. Read through old journal entries. A forgotten notation might trigger an article or story idea.

Pitfalls Along the Way

Despite all their good intentions, some people with writing ability will fail as writers. Here are some pitfalls to watch for on your way to becoming a successful writer.

1. Because writers are creative people, some think they can make up their own formats and not follow the accepted, usual method. Beginning writers especially need to go by the rules, as editors are too busy to redo creative manuscripts. Be as creative as you can be while writing, but then put what you have written into the correct manuscript format and follow the proven methods for submission.

2. Some people want the fame but not the work. They have a picture in their minds of successful writers signing autographs at the local bookstore, jetting across the country for speaking engagements, or otherwise enjoying their fame. They do not go behind the scenes and observe the long, lonely hours of research, writing, and rewriting that got them their fame and fortune. In fact, most writers do not experience the fame and fortune of celebrity status. Like any profession, you see the few at the top and not the vast majority who,

without much recognition, do most of the writing that is published. And even the very successful writers spend the majority of their time at the typewriter or word processor, not out signing autographs.

3. Some people do not realize that writing is WORK. If you are not willing to put in the time necessary, you will not be successful. They think all there is to being successful is writing the first draft. If you have this idea, you will never make it as a writer. Unless you are willing to revise, you will not be successful.

I once had a student who had some talent for poetry writing and probably could have sold some if she had been willing to rewrite. She once wrote a poem that I thought, with a little revision, might sell. However, when I suggested a few minor changes you would have thought I had suggested she cut off her right arm without benefit of anesthetic. She had written those words and she wasn't about to change them. She will not make it as a writer because she will not revise.

4. Some people cannot take constructive criticism. However, to be a successful writer you have to learn to accept criticism or you will not grow and achieve your full writing potential. You need the counsel of others. If you are fortunate enough to be in a good writers' critique group, listen to their comments and act on them. Also, if an editor takes the time to write you a personal note, pay very close attention. These are very busy people and there must be something worthwhile in your manuscript if he or she took the time to comment on it. Also, it is necessary to keep in mind that it is *your writing* that is being criticized—not you as a person.

5. In a similar vein, some people stop writing after getting one rejection slip. Don't let rejection get you down. If you have really done your homework and edited and polished until your article or

story is the best it can be, don't give up. One rejection is not failure. Successful writers will tell you that they could paper their houses with the rejection slips they have received. Rejection comes with the territory. Good salesmen don't quit because one person doesn't want to buy their products. In fact, salesmen are considered successful if they sell to ten percent of their contacts. You have to learn not to take rejection personally, but to send the manuscript back out to another market. Some articles and stories sell after thirty or forty rejections. Don't give up after one!

6. Some people fail because they don't learn everything they can about the writing business. They read one article or book and become instant experts. You can always learn something new about your craft. Read all the books on writing and writing periodicals you can. Take notes and absorb the information. Attend writing conferences and learn from professionals.

7. Some people fail to become successful writers because they don't persist. Some people have articles or stories published right away, while others receive rejection slips for years before getting something published. If you want to be a successful writer you have to keep at it even when you are the only person who believes in you. Lucille Ball's mother once signed her up for acting lessons. After the first lesson, the teacher refunded her mother's money saying Lucille had absolutely no acting ability. Fortunately, Lucille and her mother disagreed and persisted.

Have the patience needed to learn from your failures and continue working until you succeed. On the other hand, don't let one success sidetrack you. You cannot claim writing success because you have had one article or story published. You have just begun, unless your writing goal was to see your name in print one time just to prove you could do it.

8. Some people fail because they start sending their manuscripts to the prestigious publications and ignore the smaller ones. I am always somewhat saddened to hear beginning writers talk about all the major publishers they are submitting to and getting rejected by. Oh, occasionally one will sell something to a major market, but most need to start with the smaller publications and work up to the bigger ones.

9. Some people fail because they say they can't afford to continue writing. You need to recognize this for the excuse it is. Most writers work full time and write part time. It is extremely difficult for anyone who is not a big name writer like Steven King or James A. Michener to earn a living writing. The average freelance writer makes around $4,000 a year—and some a lot less. Freelance writing cannot be classified as a get-rich-quick scheme.

Copyright and the Writer

Probably one of the most misunderstood and confusing aspects of freelance writing is the copyright law. We are confused about our rights and how much we can use of someone else's writing without infringing on their rights.

First, let's briefly examine copyright ownership. If you have copyright ownership, you own and control *all rights* to what you have written. It is yours to do with as you please. You can sell it, give it away, make photocopies, whatever you wish. It is yours.

Over the years you may have heard copyright law horror stories. Fortunately, we no longer are tormented by outmoded regulations. The 1976 copyright law states that as soon as your work is in tangible form, out of your head and onto paper or disk, it is copyrighted and you own it. Sound simple? Shocking as it is, the government actually wrote something sensible and easy to understand.

Because you own the copyright, you can transfer it to someone else, such as when you sell all rights to a publisher. Now *they* own the copyright. There are other instances when you transfer ownership, but this is the most common one.

Work for Hire

Beware of work-for-hire provisions in a contract. Work for hire usually occurs when an employee writes something in the regular course of his employment. This would include newspaper reporters and others who write under contract for an employer. In these cases the employer, not the employee, owns the copyright.

A few publishers still include a work-for-hire clause in contracts and they then own all rights. The decision to sell all rights is an individual one, and you will have to decide if the pay or prestige of being published in that particular publication warrants selling all rights. Just remember, once you sell all rights, your writing belongs to the publisher who bought it. You do not own any part of it.

Public Domain

Anything that is published without copyright protection or was published so long ago that the copyright has expired is in public domain. To determine if a piece is old enough to be in public domain, subtract seventy-five years from the current year (for example, 1991-75 = 1916). If it was copyrighted in that year or before it is now in public domain. Also, the United States government does not copyright its publications, so they automatically are in public domain. This makes them great places to do research.

When something is in public domain, anyone is free to use as much of it as they want without permission. This is why it is important to include a copyright symbol with the year you originally wrote it and your legal name, on your manuscript. This is especially important when submitting to a noncopyrighted publication. These are usually small publications and their masthead and entry in writers' market guides will usually indicate they are not copyrighted.

Most magazines automatically copyright each edition of their entire publication, and your article or story is protected under that copyright. However, when submitting to noncopyrighted publications, be sure to request that they place the copyright symbol and your name with your article or story.

Copyright Notice

The copyright notice consists of three parts: the copyright symbol ©, or the word *copyright*, or its abbreviation *copr.*; the year it was first published or created, if it is not yet published; and the name of the copyright owner, usually you.

All publicly distributed copies of any work published under the authority of the copyright owner should include a copyright notice.

Fair Use

Fair use refers to the amount of material you can quote from a copyrighted source without obtaining permission or making payment to the owner. The quotation used cannot infringe on another's copyright. This can be confusing as it is impossible to say exactly how many words constitute fair use. For example, a quote of 250 words from a full-length book would probably not infringe on the owner's copyright unless it includes the main premise of the book. However, if you quote 250 words from a 1,000 word article or story, you have taken one-fourth of the author's material and this would be considered copyright infringement. Also, because poems and songs are quite short, any use without permission is considered a copyright infringement. The best rule is: If in doubt, ask permission.

For your information, Section 107 of Title 17, *United States Code* is reprinted here in full:

> s107. Limitations on exclusive rights: Fair use Notwithstanding the provisions of Section 106, the fair use of a copyrighted work, including such use by reproduction in copies or phonorecords or by any other means specified by that section, for purposes such as criticism, comment, news reporting, teaching (including multiple copies for classroom use), scholarship, or research, is not an infringement of copyright. In determining whether the use made of a work in any particular case is a fair use the factors to be considered shall include—
>
> (1) the purpose and character of the use, including whether such use is of a commercial nature or is for nonprofit educational purposes;
>
> (2) the nature of the copyrighted work;
>
> (3) the amount and substantiality of the portion used in relation to the copyrighted work as a whole; and
>
> (4) the effect of the use upon the potential market for or value of the copyrighted work.

Plagiarism

Plagiarism is something every conscientious writer wants to avoid. Plagiarism is representing someone else's writing as your own. This is not the same as using their material with permission or within the limitations of the fair use law. This is using it and not saying where it came from or even that it was quoted. In other words, you are passing off someone else's words as your own.

Recently there have been some high publicity lawsuits involving plagiarism. It can be quite a costly proposition and, at the very least, can cost you your reputation for being reliable and trustworthy. In 1988, Joe Biden lost his chance to run for President of the United States upon disclosure that he had plagiarized a paper in college.

Trademarks and Brand Names

Our language is constantly changing. If you think it isn't, try reading something written in Old or even Middle English. New words are constantly being added. Some new words come from fiction. For example, *quixotic* means "a visionary" and comes from the novel *Don Quixote.* Words like this are quite acceptable. However, words that are derived from products or names of services may infringe on a company's trademark. In fact, some have been used generically so long that they are no longer recognized as having once been a proper noun, such as: escalator, nylon, mimeograph. Companies are so concerned about protecting their trademarks that they sometimes run full page ads in writers' magazines alerting writers to the misuse.

Probably the one in greatest danger at this time is *Xerox,* a registered trademark of the Xerox Corporation. Almost everyone has said he is going to *Xerox* a paper. When used this way the term becomes synonymous with photocopying.

Just as we want people to protect and respect our copyrights, we need to protect and respect company brand names and trademarks. Whenever you are using a term that you think might be a trademark or brand name, check and then use the appropriate symbol with it.

Examples: Post-it™, Rolodex®, Kleenex®.

White Space

White space is just what it sounds like. It is the amount of white on a page. For example, a page of dialogue has a lot more white space than one containing lengthy paragraphs of narration. Study publications and notice the amount of white space they use. Readers like white space. It makes them think the reading is going to be easy.

Have you ever picked up a magazine or book and been greeted by lengthy paragraphs with little white space? What is your reaction? I know mine often is to go on to something that looks less tedious and time consuming. If you find the pages of your manuscript do not contain much white space, look for ways to break lengthy paragraphs into two or even three shorter ones—or change some narration to dialogue.

Honing Your Writing Skills

Good writers never stop learning. Read, read, read. Mark Twain once observed: "The man who does not read good books has no advantage over the man who can't read them." Read books on writing and writers' magazines. Attend writers' conferences. These are terrific places to renew your commitment to writing, get encouragement from other writers, and make valuable contacts with editors. Join an instructional writers' group; one that brings in speakers, offers critiques, shares marketing information, and helps you improve your skills.

To be a successful freelance writer, you must make time to write, even if you can squeeze only thirty minutes to an hour a day. Or you may be able to set aside larger chunks of time two or three times a week. Don't let the outside world intrude on that time. Get an answering machine or unplug the telephone, if necessary.

Writing is a process of inquiry and of discovery. As writers, we search for meaning and the proper form to convey it most effectively to our readers. We use our basic writing skills to create something that is truly our own. We focus our writing, decide what we want to tell our readers, and say it effectively.

Above all, we must write, write, write.

Chapter 2:

Before You Begin

When writing you may mentally divide your article or story into three parts: the lead, the middle, and the end. Likewise, the process of writing can be divided into three parts: prewriting, writing, and rewriting. While you probably will find disagreement among professional writers over which part is the most important, most agree that the better job of prewriting you do, the easier writing and rewriting will be.

Prewriting includes all the preparations you make before starting to write: deciding on a topic, thinking about it, reading about it, gathering information, and planning what to write. It even might include discussing your ideas with someone who will listen sympathetically and give you some good feedback.

Research

Since good writing comes from an abundance of information, professional writers often spend as much as ten times as much time researching a topic as they do actually writing. While they may not directly use most of the information, it is there for them to draw on as they write. If you have only done enough research to get by, your writing will lack depth.

Your information comes from both direct and vicarious experiences. The direct experiences are what you have actually learned from living, while the vicarious ones are what you learn from others. They may come from reading, interviewing, studying, or watching.

For example, if you are planning to write a historical novel set in the early 1800s in Arizona, and the farthest west you have been is Pennsylvania, you have your prewriting homework cut out for you. Not only do you need to learn all you can about life in the early 1800s, but you need to get a feel for life in Arizona: its climate, its terrain, its accents. If possible, visit there as there is nothing like firsthand experience to get you acquainted with the area. Elaine L. Schulte wrote a romance series set in the 1800s in which her characters traveled from New York to Missouri and then on to California. To do her research, she traveled to the various locales where she was setting her story.

In addition, your characters must be products of their time. Therefore, you must research their time so you will know how they walked and talked and reacted. Readers today are much more sophisticated than they used to be and will check your writing for accuracy. Your details *must* be accurate.

Mrs. Schulte states that when getting ready to write a camp meeting scene set in 1840, she went through old hymnals to be sure the songs she included were ones actually sung in that era. She also read sermons of the period to get the feel for the words and phrasing the preacher would have used.

In addition, to help keep readers oriented in time, the conflicts should evolve from historical events or known customs of the time and place you have chosen. When historical romance writer Esther Loewen Vogt read accounts of a small German Dunker church that had been in the midst of the Battle of Antietam during the Civil War, she decided to use it in a story. Using the Civil War and the conflict that must have gone on in the pacifist members' minds, she wrote *The Splendid Vista.*

Of course, you need to do research whether you are writing a contemporary or historical novel, a short story, or a piece of nonfiction. Very little writing can be done well without some research. Whatever size town you live in, your local library is a good starting place for your research. In addition, if you have a computer and modem and access to an online database, you can research almost any topic you wish without leaving home.

After researching your general topic, you must get it into manageable form. As you prepare to write, several brainstorming techniques can help you organize your thoughts.

Brainstorming

Any of you who remember *The Dick Van Dyke Show* saw Rob, Sally, and Buddy brainstorming as they tried to come up with comedy routines. While brainstorming can be done in a group, it also can be done quite well individually. As you brainstorm, write down as many thoughts about your article or story as you can. You are after quantity, not quality. In fact, one of the keys to effective brainstorming is to let your thoughts flow freely without editing them as you go. If you stop to analyze what you have written, you will squelch the creative flow. Granted, some of what you are writing will have nothing to do with your subject, but if you stop the flow you will miss some really creative ideas.

Even when you think all your ideas are exhausted, don't give up. Simply switch to another mode of thought. Switch into sensory mode and think about things related to your subject that you can see, hear, feel, touch, or taste. Call upon memories that are related to it. Or reflect on (think over) ideas associated with your subject. Just keep writing. Continue to shift your focus until ideas and details begin to flow again. If a particular topic seems to be working, stick with it and record as many specific details as possible before going on to another.

Make up questions you think your readers might ask and information they might want to know. Write the main idea on a piece of paper, then ask yourself questions about it: What words need to be defined? What do I mean? How can I illustrate or support the topic? How is it like, or different from, other things? Can I compare it to something in a different class that's more familiar to my readers using allegory? What makes it work?

Then answer the questions with specific information. Write down all the ideas, facts, examples, and anecdotes that come to mind. This not only will help you organize your information, but if you haven't researched a particular aspect enough, you will know at this stage.

When thinking about your topic, another method to generate ideas is to give yourself five, ten, or at the most fifteen minutes to write about it. Again, write anything you can think of relating to it, perhaps experiences or quotations, or random thoughts. As with brainstorming, write constantly without criticizing what you have written until you reach your time limit. You might set a timer bell so you won't be distracted wondering how long you've been writing.

Or, rather than setting a specific time limit, you could force yourself to fill up a certain number of pages about the subject. Don't, however, set a number that will discourage you. One or two pages is enough.

The following questions can help you organize the ideas and details you have acquired through your brainstorming:

1. What ones have something in common? What is it? You can use the common element as a heading.

2. Are some of the items within the group more important than others? If so, star or otherwise mark them.

3. Which of the items are subdivisions of main points? They could be examples, statistics, or quotes. In fact, if you find you do not have any subdivisions, you need to return to the research stage as you do not have enough information yet.

4. Do you have some items that do not fit within the groupings? Put them aside. They are not needed for the present project, but keep them so they can be used later for another topic.

Next, group your ideas into broad patterns. As you organize your ideas, put them in a logical order and you will be able to get rid of those not directly connected with your topic. Here again, you may find areas that need additional research.

Sentence completion is a good idea starter. Try to complete any open-ended sentence in as many ways as you can. As you write your sentences, try to word them so they can lead to something you might be able to use later.

Ideas: I wonder how...; What would happen if...; It really makes me angry when...; It really makes me happy when..., and so on.

Always be on the lookout for writing ideas. They turn up in the most unexpected places. An unusual event, person, object, or conversation may trigger your next article or story idea.

Vary your experiences. Most of us tend to stay with what we know because it is comfortable. Get out of that rut. Have a new experience even if it is as mundane as trying a new dish at your favorite restaurant. Go to an ethnic restaurant you've never tried before. Record your impressions of the experience.

If you write nonfiction, you need to keep up with the trends of the day. One way to do this is to watch the news and read the daily newspaper and news magazines. You also can check the current topics in the vertical files in the public library or look at the current headings in *Readers' Guide to Periodical Literature*.

If you have already done most of your research or are already somewhat familiar with your topic, you might try writing several different introductions. If you are writing nonfiction, you will want to whet your readers' appetite for your subject. If you are writing fiction, you will want to hook them by making them want to know what is going to happen next.

Think of a variety of ways to approach your topic. Of course, this is tied into audience and purpose, which we will discuss in detail in Chapter 3, but even after you have decided that, you still will have several options for dealing effectively with the topic. Write some down and then revise them as many ways as you can.

By now, you should have your ideas narrowed down to one or two that you will be able to handle. What do you do with the rest of your prewriting exercises? No, no! Do not file them in the circular file! You have too much time and work invested in them. Besides, you never know when one of them can be used for another article or story. File them where you will be able to find them later.

As you finish the prewriting process sum up your idea in just a sentence or two. If you are unable to do this, you do not have a narrow enough focus or a clear enough plot in mind.

If possible, give your ideas a chance to simmer on the back burner of your mind for a while. A study of the creative processes of artists and scientists underscores the importance of this simmering time. They think about the problem, get a few ideas, and then set the problem aside and work on another project. Often the solution will come to them at an unexpected time as the subconscious mind is working on it even when the conscious is thinking about something else. This setting aside gives a fresh perspective on the problem. While your conscious mind is thinking about other matters, your subconscious is busily trying to solve the dilemma. Once I awoke at 4:00 a.m. with the solution to a problem that had been bothering me for weeks.

Probably one of the most famous examples of percolating thought is the story told about the mathematician Archimedes (287-212 B.C.). Hieron II, ruler of Syracuse, had asked Archimedes to determine whether base metal had been added when his golden crown was made. Archimedes thought about the problem for a long time and could not come up with a solution without melting down the crown. Then, one day as he observed the water in his bath being displaced by his body, the answer came to him. He could test the crown by specific gravity. It is said that in his excitement he rushed naked through the streets joyfully shouting "Eureka!"

While I doubt any of us will become that excited, it is exhilarating when an answer comes unexpectedly.

Once you have your prewriting research done, it is time to make a final decision about your audience, purpose, and tone.

Chapter 3:

Tone, Audience, and Purpose

When most people think of tone, they think of actual sound, possibly music. However, writing also has tone. Writing tone is how writers express ideas and how the words sound to the readers' minds. Tone is what is transferred to readers. Good writers know how to control tone so it agrees with their purpose for writing.

Tone may be serious or humorous, formal or informal, mysterious or candid. But whatever tone you choose, what you write and how you write it will determine whether you are able to reproduce it in your readers' minds. If you can, you'll be communicating effectively. Choosing the right words will transfer a clear mental picture.

Tone, audience, and purpose are so closely related that they must be considered together. Audience and purpose directly affect the tone of writing.

Audience Affects Tone

As you set out to determine your audience, don't fall into the trap of thinking you can write something everyone will want to read. There is no such thing as a generic article or story.

As you think about your audience you need to ask yourself some questions:

1. What is its general age group?

2. What is their educational background?

3. What are their interests?

4. How interested will they be in my subject?

5. What is their relationship to me, the writer?

The age of your audience will affect your tone. If you are writing to young children, you will use a more informal tone and a simpler vocabulary than if you are writing for teens or adults.

Example:

> Mario and Ted were the engineer and fireman aboard a freight train. Sometimes the engine pulled more than a hundred cars. The freight train had a caboose. It was the conductor's office. Frank was the conductor on Mario's train.
>
> ["The Long Freight Train" by Campbell Tatham.]

Then, it is important to know the educational background of your audience. Today a sixth- to eighth-grade vocabulary is used when writing for a general adult audience. However, if you know your audience is mainly college-educated, you would use a more extensive vocabulary, and, depending on the topic, a more formal tone.

What are your intended audience's interests? Even an audience narrowed to adults, still offers much diversity. That's why you must know exactly who they are. For example, if you are planning to write for a magazine, you need to be aware of its slant, its style, and its readership. The magazine's slant tells you what position it will accept on controversial issues. In addition, some magazines have their own distinct tone. Another reason to know who the readers are is so your articles or stories can meet their needs. For instance, a sports magazine would not publish a love story, nor would a women's magazine publish an article on fly fishing.

What interest will your intended audience have in your subject? If you are researching an article on the latest cancer breakthrough, you will give different information to a group of health professionals than to a more general audience. In an article to health professionals you would include technical information and terms, as well as information on how they can use the breakthrough to help their patients who have cancer. On the other hand, the general public's main interest is how it is going to help them or a loved one in their fight against cancer.

Of course, the tone is affected by whom you are discussing the topic with and the situation. You would use one tone when ironing out a serious disagreement with your boss, but would use another telling a friend your problems.

If you are writing nonfiction, here are some questions you need to ask yourself about your intended audience:

1. What information do they already have about the subject? You would not include background information about the Kentucky Derby if your main audience was from Louisville, Kentucky.

2. Is there background or technical information they might need to understand the subject? If they know very little about your topic, you need to explain in detail so they will not be confused when they finish reading.

3. What style of writing is most appropriate for your audience and topic? Should you use simple or complex language and sentence structure? Should you use a formal or informal tone?

4. If you are writing on a potentially controversial subject, does your intended audience have any bias or strong feelings either for or against your subject? If so, what? How will that affect your writing? If your audience holds a strongly opposing view, you are probably wasting your time trying to change their minds.

5. Ask yourself the five W's and H questions: Who, what, where, why, when, and how.

By now you should have a pretty clear picture of who your audience is. Next, you need to decide what kind of relationship you will have with them. If you want to develop a close relationship with your audience and reveal some of your personality to them, you will use first person pronouns, I, me, we, us. This creates a closeness and draws your audience closer to you.

On the other hand, third person pronouns such as *he, she, they,* create a distance between you and your readers. This greater distance puts more emphasis on the subject and less on you, the writer.

Determine The Purpose

Now that you have defined your audience, turn to your reason, or purpose, for writing. Purpose has been defined as the writer's controlling decision about what he is going to do and how he is going to do it. While you have probably been thinking about it already, it is time to get it into clear focus. Are you going to entertain, inform, or persuade? Just what do you want your readers to know or do when they have finished reading?

Your purpose will affect your choice of words and will create the desired tone. For example, to entertain an audience, use a light, humorous tone and words like carnival, carousel, clown, and circus. However, to discuss the causes of war, use a more formal and serious tone and words like death, destruction, hunger, hatred, and homeless.

If you are writing an expository article, you will use an objective and informative tone to teach your readers something, or to help them reach a higher level of understanding than they had before. Because you are teaching your readers, you will want to present the information and ideas in a clear and unbiased manner. You can create an informative tone by defining terms and giving clear, concise explanations. You would have an instructional purpose in mind.

You want to be sure to choose the most accurate words possible and be sure they are ones your readers should understand. Here, again, the importance of knowing your audience is apparent as you need to know their background and their knowledge of the topic.

Let's say you are going to explain how a computer works to someone who doesn't even have a clue where the on switch is. You would use very basic language and explain terms thoroughly. On the other hand, if you were going to explain the latest technical advance

to a group of computer programmers, you would use much more
technical terms and language, possibly even jargon.

In persuasive writing you want a mutual identification with your
readers. Anything that increases the distance between you and your
readers decreases your chances of convincing them of your point of
view. The safest thing to do is to treat your readers with respect but
with as much intimacy as the situation permits. However, be careful
not to talk down to them but to treat them as equals. The tone also
will vary depending on the importance and urgency of the topic and
how strongly you feel about it. Be careful not to use words with
either strongly negative or strongly positive connotations. Also, do
not include unsupported opinions or emotionally charged words. All
of these will distort your intended tone.

Specific, concrete language will help create a persuasive tone
and add interest and information. And, depending on the topic, language may be humorous or serious and formal or informal. However,
whatever tone you choose, be sure it is always reasonable.

You must plan carefully when making decisions about your purpose. Writing is much more difficult if you do not have a clear purpose. You face decisions including what material to use, how to
organize it, what words to choose, and what style to use. A clear purpose will make those decisions easier and editing will be less frustrating. You will know what you are trying to accomplish and can
examine your writing to see if you are fulfilling your goals.

By the time you have determined your audience and purpose
you should have a clear idea of what tone to use. Remember, your
tone expresses your attitude toward the readers and the topic under
discussion.

Keeping The Correct Tone

After you have determined the appropriate tone, be sure to maintain it throughout your article or story. A change in tone within the body of writing upsets your audience.

The following paragraph has a tone change in the middle, which can be confusing.

> My little sister, Susan, is quite a character. I never know what she is going to do next. Just the other day she climbed up on a chair and got all of Mom's make-up out. What a mess! Susan is thirty-three inches tall and weighs thirty-five pounds, average for a two-year-old. She has light brown hair and blue eyes.

In the middle of the above paragraph the tone went from casual and informal to formal and clinical. The writer could, however, give the same information and still maintain the intended tone. Here is a revision.

> My two-year-old sister, Susan, is thirty-five pounds of pure dynamite. Things are never dull when she's around. Just the other day, with mischief dancing in her blue eyes, she climbed up on a chair and got all of Mom's make-up out. What a mess! She had it everywhere! Mom had a terrible time washing it out of Susan's shoulder-length, light-brown hair. You wouldn't think someone who is only thirty-three inches tall could get into so much trouble. But, then, you don't know Susan!

Appropriate Choices

However, maintaining tone is not enough, it must be appropriate for the situation. For instance, when writing to the president of a bank to ask for a loan you would not start the letter: "Hi, Fred, how's it going?" Or, if you were writing about the mayor's hospitalization for heart by-pass surgery, you wouldn't write: "The mayor's *ticker* was on the *blink*." These situations require more formal language.

On the other hand, to get help cleaning out the garage, you would not ask for "assistance in disposing of refuse." You would want "help in throwing out the trash."

So, your tone depends on the subject and situation as well as the audience and purpose.

Formal vs. Informal Style

Tone also is affected by differences between a formal and an informal writing style. For instance, formal writing normally uses a more extensive, specific, and technical vocabulary than informal. Formal will say *arduous* instead of *difficult* and *precarious* instead of *risky.*

Formal writing also is more likely to maintain the traditional distinctions between pairs like *who* and *whom, can* and *may,* and *if he were* and *if he was.* Formal writing will not use contractions like *don't* and *isn't,* while informal will. And, the transitions used in formal are likely to be more obvious than in informal, such as *however, moreover,* and *nevertheless.*

In addition, the organization of formal writing is likely to be more structured than informal. Within formal paragraphs both agreeing and opposing ideas probably will use parallel construction.

Parallel structure puts similar ideas into the same kinds of grammatical constructions. If one idea in a sentence is expressed by a phrase, other equal ideas are expressed by phrases. If one idea is expressed by an infinitive, a gerund, or a clause, other equal ideas are expressed by duplicate grammatical constructions.

Examples:

1. The fault, dear Brutus, is not *in our stars,* but *in ourselves.*

2. The work of a copyeditor is *to correct* spelling, capitalization, and punctuation; *to use* proper grammar and punctuation; and *to do* a variety of production-related tasks.

Formal writing may have several clearly labeled subdivisions in a very logical order and be easy to outline. On the other hand, informal writing often is loosely structured and may be difficult to outline. Informal unity usually comes from an underlying mood.

Formal writing also uses a wider range of allusions and comparisons than informal, as well as references to history, literature, and the fine arts. Such references are not explained because readers are expected to understand "Napoleonic airs," "Pyrrhic victory," or the feel of the "Procrustean bed."

On the other hand, informal writing allusions and comparisons are likely to be ones the average person will understand without explanation. They will be about home, sports, or work. Informal writing may contain personal impressions or reminiscences by the writer. Readers often learn as much about the author as about the subject.

Another difference is sentence structure. In formal writing, sentence structure generally is more complex than for informal. Formal sentences often use a series of grammatically parallel elements, while informal sentences often use a one subject, one verb pattern. In addition, a minor point or short comment in formal writing may appear as a parenthetic observation in a sentence, while in informal it may be in a sentence by itself.

Formal Example with parallel construction:

The day of my father's funeral had also been my nineteenth birthday. As we drove him to the graveyard, the spoils of injustice, anarchy, discontent, and hatred were all around us. It seemed to me that God himself had devised, to mark my father's end, the most sustained and brutally dissonant of codas. And it seemed to me,

too, that the violence which rose all about us as my father left the
world had been devised as a corrective for the pride of his eldest
son. I had declined to believe in that apocalypse which had been
central to my father's vision; very well, life seemed to be saying,
here is something that will certainly pass for an apocalypse until
the real thing comes along. I had inclined to be contemptuous of
my father for the conditions of his life, for the conditions of our
lives. When his life had ended I began to wonder about that life
and also, in a new way, to be apprehensive about my own.

["Notes of a Native Son," by James Baldwin]

Formal Example with parenthetic observation:

Now, the settlers brought out from Europe, more specifically
from the British Isles, this aristocratic culture. (The Bible, after
all, is full of kings and nobles, sinners most of them, but interesting
sinners. The metaphorical language of the Bible is royal, not
democratic.) But in the American environment the aristocratic
culture, accepted and admired by the people, began to wither. The
old ballads were brought over but were transformed, given an
American, frontier-bred, forest-bred character. The legends of
kings and princes became legends of men of the people winning
the endless war against the wilderness and the Indian. Robin Hood
was a hero that could be transported to the frontier; Richard Coeur
de Lion was not.

["The Character of American Culture" by D.W. Brogan]

Informal Example:

But here I was, crouched in my vision pit, left alone by
myself for the first time in my life. I was sixteen then, still had my
boy's name and, let me tell you, I was scared. I was shivering and
not only from the cold. The nearest human being was many miles
away, and four days and nights is a long, long time. Of course,
when it was all over, I would no longer be a boy, but a man. I
would have had my vision. I would be given a man's name.

["Alone on the Hilltop" by John Fire/Lame Deer, from *Lame Deer:
Seeker of Visions* by John Fire/Lame Deer and Richard Erdos]

In formal writing, everyone — writer, reader, and people in general — may be referred to by the impersonal one. "One cannot but..." or "One tends to..." However, informal writing often uses the first person, *I* or *we*, and second person, *you*. "I cannot but..." or "You tend to..."

When making a point in a formal argument the writer will usually maintain an objective, detached tone even when presenting a personal comment. Her conclusions and opinions also will stay close to the evidence she has presented. On the other hand, a writer using an informal tone may become more closely associated with the subject and tell you when she is expressing her opinion.

Yet, despite their differences, the line between formal and informal is not always easy to define. It often is one of shading, with some expressions sounding more casual or informal than others.

Tone Problems

Next, let's look at words that can destroy your desired tone. When you find them, throw them out.

Slang

Slang can easily sneak into your writing. Slang consists of popular words and phrases used by certain age groups or in certain regions of the country. While everyone in the particular group will understand what you mean, someone else would not. In addition, slang expressions usually are vague and imprecise. They often are dependent upon a speaker's intonation and expression. And, they may depend on sentence context to make sense. Thus, you risk tone distortion and being misunderstood when you use slang.

Example using slang:

The roundballers were really fired up for the tourney.

While many teens would understand the sentence, a more general audience might not. The following example is much clearer and avoids any possible confusion.

Better written:

> The basketball team had practiced hard and was ready to play for the state championship.

Also, slang tends to be short-lived. Since we all hope for longevity for our writing, we don't want to use words that immediately date it.

Jargon

Yet another hindrance to clear writing is jargon. The term comes from a middle French word meaning "a chattering of birds." Jargon is the technical language of a specific group, e.g., doctors, lawyers, ham radio operators, yes, even writers. If you happen to be writing for such a group, its jargon is acceptable. However, the general public will have little or no idea what you are discussing.

Walter Kaufmann, philosopher, says this about jargon: "Men love jargon. It is so palpable, tangible, visible, audible; it makes so obvious what one has learned; it satisfies the craving for results. It is impressive for the uninitiated. It makes one feel that one belongs. Jargon divides men into Us and Them."

Jargon can cause tone problems and loss of clarity. It is irritating to read an article written in an unfamiliar jargon. For example, the following paragraph makes little sense to anyone not familiar with ham radio operation:

> In the same manner, the combination of U3c, U7b, and Q1 control the Receive Hold Function of the Scan Can. Q1 serves as a buffer switch and interfaces with the receive LED of the KDK. A 2-volt potential on the base of Q1 forces the collector to go low.

> When U7b pins 5 and 6 are L, the pin 4 of U7b goes H. When U3b
> pin 12 is H, then the counter U4 stops counting and holds. How-
> ever, when zero volts is on the base of Q1, the counter resumes
> counting. When the scan function is in the Receive Hold condition
> and S2 pin 1 is placed to an L, the scan is resumed.
>
> [*73 for Radio Amateurs*, February, 1986, page 37.]

Carefully check your writing for jargon. In fact, you will benefit from someone unacquainted with the topic reading your article to point out any unfamiliar terms.

Here are some suggestions when using technical terms:

1. Determine how much your intended audience knows about the subject.

2. Do not introduce too many new technical terms. People need time to absorb new ideas and can't handle too many too fast.

3. Only use terms necessary for a systematic discussion of your topic. Stifle

the desire to use them merely to impress your readers with your superior knowledge.

4. If you think your readers may not understand some of the terms be sure to clarify or explain them. Or, better yet, put the information in language you know they will understand.

Terms belonging to a limited group make a wider audience feel left out. Unless the intended audience is familiar with the jargon, leave it out.

Euphemisms

Euphemisms also destroy tone. These are words or phrases used to soften a fact that someone does not want to face. Some euphemisms are harmless, for example, *senior citizen* or *elderly* sometimes are substituted for *old.* Others are used to hide a truth the writer does not want readers to understand. This is dishonest and poor journalism.

In recent years American businesses have perfected the use of euphemisms to the point that it has been labeled "doublespeak." When a business wants to sound fancier than it really is or hide what it actually is doing, it resorts to doublespeak, intending to totally confuse the general public.

For example, a business recession in the automobile industry was referred to by one executive as "a period of negative economic growth." And no longer will any UPS driver have the dubious distinction of being the worst driver in the company; he now will be the "least-best" driver. In 1988 North American Van Lines stopped being a moving company and became "North American Relocation Services." An auto junkyard has become "auto dismantlers and recyclers" who sell "predismantled, previously owned parts." Doublespeak is another example of fuzzy writing caused by euphemisms, and needs to be avoided in the quest for clear communication.

When you find euphemisms in your writing, remove them. You don't want the insincere tone and confusion they can cause.

Emotional Language

Emotional language also causes trouble. It includes words that express strong, often unsupported opinions. It yells at the audience, causing readers to be immediately on the defensive. It also sours your tone by making it offensive and insulting. For example, calling someone a "freeloading low-life" does not get the point across. However, "He is usually late to work, takes two-hour lunch breaks, and sleeps on the job," gives concrete examples and will convince readers there is a problem.

Emotional language sometimes will creep into persuasive writing, as we usually feel strongly about our topic. However, you will lose the argument if you leave it in. You need to go on a search and destroy mission. You will prove your point much faster with calm, well thought out language.

Word Connotations

As you choose your words, you must be careful when using words that can mean more than one thing. While the denotation of a word is its literal dictionary definition, connotations are broader meanings. They include suggested meanings and associations. Some words are neutral, others negative, and still others have strongly negative connotations. For a further discussion of word connotations, see chapter 11, "Getting Specific."

Self-Important Language

Finally, be careful not to use self-important language which uses a better-than-thou tone. Self-important language attempts to sound impressive by using long, vague, and unfamiliar words. It may contain too many adjectives and adverbs or include vague, general nouns, or long verbs ending in -ate or -ize.

Example:

> If one will familiarize one's self with the assorted materials available, it will facilitate one becoming accustomed to this company's procedures in transacting business.

A rewrite:

> If you will look over the available materials, it will help you learn how we operate our company.

Sentence Structure Affects Tone

Your choice of sentence structure can help create the desired tone. *Extracurricular activities are a waste of time,* makes a short, concise statement of the person's opinion and plants an unfavorable impression of extracurricular activities in readers' minds. On the other hand, *To become a well-adjusted person, a student should participate in extracurricular activities,* creates a tone sympathetic to extracurricular activities. The longer sentence, beginning with an introductory explanation, sets a more positive tone.

Set the Tone Immediately

As you start writing, you must set the tone immediately for your reader. Notice how these two opening nonfiction paragraphs dealing with the subject of bee stings, lets readers know the writer's purpose.

Informal, humorous essay:

> I love nature, but I do think it can be overdone. There is so much sympathy for dumb animals along Hunting Ridge that human rights are neglected. Yesterday, for instance, I was stung by a bee and everybody around blamed me. There was much indignation when I killed him, even though I exhibited the bite and pleaded self-defense.

Formal, informational essay:

> The sting apparatus [of the bee] is made up of a poison sack, located in the abdomen and connected with a sheath. The sting, which is a double-bladed spear with barbed edges, passes in and out of this sheath at will; and the venom from the poison sack runs between these two blades and into the pin-prick opening the blades for it.

The following opening paragraphs show how three well-known writers set their stories' tone immediately:

Humorous:

> It was the best of times.
>
> I had my own watch, a tricycle, and a clip-on Shirley Temple hair ribbon that covered the entire right side of my head. My mother wore an apron and silk stockings and baked every day. She looked like Betty Crocker looked before her face-lift, pierced ears and junk to make her hair fat.
>
> [Erma Bombeck, *Family: The Ties That Bind...And Gag!*]

Somber:

> The "Red Death" had long devastated the country. No pestilence had ever been so fatal or so hideous. Blood was its Avatar and its seal—the redness and horror of blood. There were sharp pains, and sudden dizziness, and then profuse bleeding at the pores, with dissolution. The scarlet stains upon the body and especially upon the face of the victim were the pest ban which shut him out from the aid and from the sympathy of his fellowmen. And the whole seizure, progress, and termination of the disease were the incidents of half an hour.
>
> [Edgar Allen Poe, "The Masque of the Red Death."]

Also, notice the many references to red and blood. Poe chose his words very carefully to set the desired tone.

Sentimental, informal:

> One dollar and eighty-seven cents. That was all. And sixty cents of it was in pennies. Pennies saved one and two at a time by bulldozing the grocer and the vegetable man and the butcher until one's cheek burned with silent imputation of parsimony that such close dealing implied. Three times Della counted it. One dollar and eight-seven cents. And the next day would be Christmas.
>
> [O. Henry, "The Gift of the Magi."]

Titles and Tone

Finally, your title can help set the tone of your article or story. For example, the title of the humorous essay on bees is "Stung!"; the more formal informative one is "The Bee Sting." Each title sets the appropriate tone for the particular essay. If you pick up Robin Cook's *Coma* or *Outbreak,* you can be sure you are going to read about a serious medical problem. On the other hand, Erma Bombeck's *If Life's a Bowl of Cherries, What Am I Doing In The Pits?* lets you know immediately that she is taking a humorous look at life.

You need to create titles that will grab your readers' attention. See chapter 7, "The Title's the Thing."

Your Turn

Now let's see if you can figure out the tone of the following opening paragraphs:

1. Mr. Monroe stood fingering some canes in a shop in the Fifties. Canes, it occurred to him, were imperturbable. He liked that adjective, which he had been encountering in a book he was reading on God, ethics, morals, humanism, and so on. The word stood staunch, like a bulwark, rumbled, like a caisson. Mr. Monroe was pleased to find himself dealing in similes.

2. The day was cloudy and gray as Sammy Squirrel padded down a path in Deep Green Wood. Dry leaves rustled in the cold wind, sounding like eerie whispers all around him.

3. Dark spruce forest frowned on either side the frozen waterway. The trees had been stripped by a recent wind of their white covering of the frost, and they seemed to lean toward each other, black and ominous, in the fading light. A vast silence reigned over the land. The land itself was a desolation, lifeless, without movement, so lone and cold that the spirit of it was not even that of sadness. There was a hint in it of laughter, but of a laughter more terrible than any sadness—a laughter that was mirthless as the smile

of the Sphinx, a laughter cold as the frost and partaking of the grimness of infallibility. It was the masterful and incommunicable wisdom of eternity laughing at the futility of life and the effort of life. It was the Wild, the savage, frozenhearted Northland Wild.

4. In compliance with the request of a friend of mine, who wrote me from the East, I called on good-natured, garrulous old Simon Wheeler, and inquired after my friend's friend, Leonidas W. Smiley, as requested to do, and I hereunto append the result. I have a lurking suspicion that *Leonidas W.* Smiley is a myth; that my friend never knew such a personage; and that he only conjectured that if I asked old Wheeler about him, it would remind him of his infamous *Jim* Smiley, and he would go to work and bore me to death with some exasperating reminiscence of him as long and as tedious as it should be useless to me. If that was the design, it succeeded.

5. I do not propose to add anything to what has already been written concerning the loss of the *Lady Vain.* As everyone knows, she collided with a derelict when ten days out of Callao. The longboat with seven of the crew was picked up eighteen days after by H.M. gun-boat *Myrtle,* and the story of their privations has become almost as well known as the far more terrible Medusa case. I have now, however, to add to the published story of the *Lady Vain* another as horrible, and certainly far stranger. It has hitherto been supposed that the four men who were in the dinghy perished, but this is incorrect. I have the best evidence for this assertion—I am one of the four men.

Answers to tones of opening paragraphs:

1. Thurber, James. "The Imperturbable Spirit" (humorous)
2. Welsh, Kathy. "Adventures of Ranger Rick," Ranger Rick, October 1989, p. 15. (simple, conversational)

3. London, Jack. White Fang. (somber)
4. Twain, Mark. "The Notorious Jumping Frog of Calaveras County" (humorous)
5. Wells, H. G. The Island of Dr. Moreau. (mysterious)

Chapter 4:

Hooking the Reader

Any fisherman can tell you that you must set the hook early if you want to get the fish out of the water and into the boat or up onto the pier. We writers also must hook our readers early to keep their attention. To do this, begin your story or article with a lead that pulls the readers into the main part. They *have* to keep reading to find out what is going to happen next. We must be aggressive. We must give the readers irresistible bait so they will bite and we can reel them in.

Put yourself in your readers' place. Ask yourself how you would react if you were looking for something to read and came upon your lead. Would you continue? Be honest. Make your lead something readers will grab onto and get hooked.

In addition to hooking your readers, your lead should give some indication of what they can expect. The lead sets the tone for what will come later. It should not mislead the reader, but focus directly on what will follow. You must create enough interest in what's coming to keep readers turning the pages.

The fiction lead should make readers eager to find out what is going to happen to the protagonist. The nonfiction lead should make readers anxious to read about the subject. However, don't give away the plot or the premise in the lead. Give just enough information to draw your readers in and keep them intrigued.

Do not, however, promise more than you can deliver. To hook the reader with a lead that indicates real conflict coming, and then deliver something ho-hum is playing unfair. For example, if you used the cliché opener "'Get your hand off my knee,' cried the duchess," something exciting had better be happening. If her doctor is examining a cut on her knee and he has hurt her, the readers will spit out the bait. But, if you have a Don Juan type resting his hand on her knee at a formal dinner, then your readers will take the bait and read on.

Likewise, the nonfiction lead that promises your readers you will teach them how to sew a dress in an afternoon, followed by complicated directions that would take at least a week to complete, is equally unfair. Or if you promised eight money-saving tips when having your car repaired, don't give them six.

Leads to Avoid

Before looking at some time-tested types of effective leads, here are some to avoid:

Proper Noun Openings: One way to bore and lose your reader is to start with a proper noun.

Example, Nonfiction:

The State Department announced plans today to have the President and the Soviet leader meet sometime next month. (Boring.)

Better: Despite the recent set-back in the arms reduction talks, plans are being finalized for a United States-Soviet Summit sometime next month.

Example, Fiction:

Diane hung up the phone and walked out of the house.

Better: Slamming the phone down, Diane stormed out of the house.

Definition Lead: A definition lead is about as exciting as a dictionary entry. The information is important, but not necessarily interesting. While you may want readers to have a clear understanding of certain terms or what a particular organization does, the lead is not the place for that information.

Definition Lead:

A Tory has been properly defined to be a traitor in thought, but not in deed.

[Thomas Jefferson, "Query XVI, Notes on Virginia"]

Definition Lead Revised:

In 1776, those who wanted to see America free of British control looked upon anyone who was a Tory as a traitor in thought.

Cliches: Avoid cliches. This is especially important, because a poorly written lead will probably discourage a busy editor from reading further. I have heard some editors say they can tell from the first page if a manuscript is going to be worth reading. If you don't grab her attention immediately, she will quickly return your manuscript to its SASE and it will never have a chance to get to your intended readers.

Cliche Lead:

> People who live in glass houses should not throw stones.

Cliche Lead with a Twist:

> People who live in wooden houses shouldn't throw rotten eggs at the neighbor's dog.

Show, Don't Tell

A common problem found in writing is telling the readers, rather than showing them what is happening. Writing that tells may be well-written, but it is boring. Writing that shows is alive and exciting.

The following paragraph introduces a character and gives important information, but is very bland and boring:

> Lisa is twenty-eight-years-old, has shoulder length auburn hair and blue eyes. She lives with her mother in a third floor apartment on Chaney Street.

We can improve the description and still give the same information in a much more interesting manner:

> Lisa quietly closed the door to the apartment and trudged down the three long flights of stairs. Never in her wildest dreams had she imagined being twenty-eight and single and still living with her mother. She sighed as she pushed back a lock of her shoulder length auburn hair. Her turquoise eyes squinted involuntarily as she stepped out into the glaring sunlight. She glanced around. "Monday morning on Chaney Street, not very exciting," she thought. She headed for the bus stop two blocks away.

We added action to the description. Readers have met Lisa, learned something about her situation, and have a partial physical description. They will read on because they will want to find out why she is in this situation.

While the following opening book paragraph is appropriate for the topic, it *tells* and does not make for exciting reading:

> No American is more completely misunderstood than George Washington. He is generally believed to have been, by birth and training, a rich, conservative, British-oriented Virginia aristocrat. As a matter of fact, he was, for the environment in which he moved, poor during his young manhood. He never set foot in England or, indeed, any part of Europe. When at seventeen he began making his own living, it was as a surveyor, defining tracts of forest on the fringes of settlement. Soon the wilderness claimed him, first as an envoy seeking out the French in frozen primeval woods and then, for almost five years, as an Indian fighter. [James Thomas Flexner, *Washington, The Indispensable Man*]

The next example shows you the locale, orients you as to when the story takes place and introduces the protagonist:

> To enter out into that silence that was the city at eight o'clock of a misty evening in November, to put your feet upon the buckling concrete walk, to step over grassy seams and make your way, hands in pockets, through the silences, that was what Mr. Leonard Mead most dearly loved to do. He would stand upon the corner of an intersection and peer down long moonlit avenues of sidewalk in four directions, deciding which way to go, but it really made no difference; he was alone in this world of A.D. 2131, or as good as alone, and with a final decision made, a path selected, he would stride off, sending patterns of frosty air before him like the smoke of a cigar.
>
> [Ray Bradbury, "The Pedestrian"]

Get to the Action

Don't overwhelm readers with background details that can be given later. Today's readers are busy people and want to get right to the action. The days are gone when you can take pages, or even chapters, getting to the main plot. I remember my disappointment when I read *Moby Dick* by Herman Melville. Because I was quite familiar with the conflict between Captain Ahab and the Great White Whale, I expected most of the book to be about that. I was disappointed to find that much of the novel dealt with the whaling industry. While whaling may be interesting to some, I was bored until Melville finally got to what I considered the main conflict.

Today's readers are not going to wait hundreds of pages for the main action. They may not even wait pages. You must get to the action immediately and work your background information in as needed to clarify what's happening. I recently overheard a high school senior say a book was boring after reading the *first paragraph*. That was all the chance he gave it to capture his attention. Back to the school library he went to get another.

Writing the Lead

The lead, in addition to being one of the most important parts of your writing, usually will be the most difficult to write. As you develop your lead you may find you have spent seventy to eighty percent of your time on it. But once you have a good solid lead the rest of your story or article will be easier to write as you have a guide pointing you in the right direction.

However, if you can't come up with a great lead, don't stop writing. Sometimes you must write a working lead and go on to the rest of the story or article. As you write the middle, an idea may come that will be just what you need for the hook. If you had sat and worried because you didn't have a lead, you would not have gotten anything written.

If you still aren't happy with your lead as you revise, quite possibly your readers won't be either. Don't despair, keep working on it. Have your spouse or a good friend read it and see if they find something you have overlooked. Take it to your writers' critique group and ask for suggestions. Good instructional groups are invaluable writing aids.

You may find the lead where you least expect it. Leads often can be found buried anywhere from the second to fifth paragraph and have been found buried as deeply as page three. We writers often ramble when writing a first draft, only discovering during revision where we have hidden our lead. While cutting out paragraphs or pages is painful, the revision process is necessary to create a marketable product.

As you think about your lead, put yourself in your readers' place. What are they thinking about? What are their concerns for the present and future? How can you meet one or more of these needs? People are me-oriented. You need to promise and deliver something for them.

Or you must create a desire or need where none exists. In *The Music Man,* Professor Harold Hill (Robert Preston) created a need for a boys' band so he could sell band instruments and uniforms. Just as a great salesman can sell a refrigerator to an Eskimo, a great writer can create a need where there was none. If there is no apparent need for your article or story, you must create one.

Some Good Leads

Your lead must be delightful, dynamic, and dazzling. It must make the reader want to continue reading. It may be an unexpected twist of a time-worn cliche, an allusion to something familiar, a hint at a mystery needing a solution, a startling fact, an anecdote, or a question that needs an answer. Whatever hook you use, if it doesn't do the job you have failed to hook your readers. They will spit out the hook and swim off in search of more tantalizing bait.

Startling fact lead:

> Suppose I began by saying that the more thickly populated an area is, the fewer animals other than man will be found living there. No doubt I should be told not to waste my reader's time by telling him that. But the truth of the matter is that the statement would be false or questionable at best.
>
> [Joseph Wood Krutch, "Conservation Is Not Enough"]

Anecdotal Leads:

Everyone likes a good story and a proven method of drawing readers in is to start with one. In fact, the anecdotal lead is probably one of the most common devices used by professional nonfiction writers. When used properly, an anecdote will capture the readers' attention and lead them on into the main text of your article.

While anecdotes are usually true stories, you can create one, if necessary, to make your point. When creating an anecdote, it should be a true-to-life scene that will help prove your point and be believable.

An interesting case study or story can be used for a nonfiction lead. I started an article about marijuana with this true story:

> Jose Hernandez was a happily married man with four children—until the night of October 18, 1981. On that fateful evening, he, his wife, and children were traveling south on I-65 just north of Crown Point, Indiana. On the 113th Street overpass stood a 17-year-old youth who had been smoking marijuana. As the Hernandez car neared the overpass the boy pushed a 24-pound concrete block off the overpass. It went through the passenger window, killing Jose instantly.

Cliché with a Twist:

While a cliché as such should not be used for a lead, a cliché with a twist can grab readers' attention. For example, "Woman works from sun to sun, but man's work is never done" will grab their attention because there is a twist they didn't expect. The women will say "wait a minute" and want to see how you came up with that "outrageous" statement. The men will say "Right on" and read on to see how you're going to prove it.

Simile or Metaphor:

A well-turned simile or metaphor also can be an attention grabber. A word of caution, however. Be careful not to mix them.

Example of mixed metaphor:

> If you fail to hook your readers, they will head for a more promising restaurant in search of a more tantalizing appetizer.

Quotation Opener:

A quotation also can grab readers' attention. You even might give it a twist by saying:

> "It is not true that a rose by any other name would smell as sweet." or "You're old enough to be my daughter."

Question Beginning:

While questions should be used carefully and sparingly, sometimes they will work. Don't, however, start with one like "What would you do if your child came home with all Fs on his report card?" Readers will have an immediate answer and won't read further. However, if you raise a thought-provoking question like: "What if it took your doctor eight years to diagnose an illness?" (That is the average time it takes to diagnose lupus.) You will reel your readers in so they can learn the answer. Even without directly asking a question, you can use your lead to raise questions in your readers' minds.

Example:

> The stooped old man moved along through the dust of an Alabama road at a curiously rapid rate. He was carrying an armful of sticks and wildflowers.
>
> [James Saxon Childers, "A Boy Who Was Traded for a Horse," the story of George Washington Carver.]

This lead raises several questions. Who is the old man? Why is he moving so rapidly? Old people are supposed to move slowly. Why is he carrying the curious combination of sticks and wildflowers?

Fiction Leads

Fiction writers can hook readers by starting with a scene that will make them want to keep reading. Tension must start immediately. Whether you have the hero hang onto the edge of a cliff as his fingers slowly lose their grip or Della recount all her money — $1.87 — on December 24th, you must create a situation that makes the readers care. They have to *want* the hero back safely on terra firma and they have to want Della to solve her dilemma.

Example:

> Walk in as though it were an ordinary travel bureau, the stranger I'd met at a bar had told me. Ask a few ordinary questions—about a trip you're planning, a vacation, anything like that. Then hint about The Folder a little, but whatever you do, don't mention it directly; wait till he brings it up himself. And if he doesn't, you might as well forget it. If you can. Because you'll never see it; you're not the type, that's all. And if you ask about it, he'll just look at you as though he doesn't know what you're talking about.
>
> [Jack Finney, "Of Missing Persons"]

Orient Your Readers

In addition, whether you are writing fiction or nonfiction, it's important to orient your reader as soon as possible to the time and place of the action. Try to work in the journalist's five W's and an H (who, what, when, where, why, and how) as soon as you can so readers won't be wondering who is doing what and where they are doing it. However, be careful to show and not tell them.

Examples:

Fiction:

> Me and Pete would go down to Old Man Killegrew's and listen to his radio. We would wait until after supper, after dark, and we would stand outside Old Man Killegrew's parlor window and we could hear it because Old Man Killegrew's wife was deaf, and so he run the radio as loud as it would run, and so me and Pete could hear it plain as Old Man Killegrew's wife could, I reckon, even standing outside with the window closed.
>
> And that night I said, "What? Japanese? What's a pearl harbor?" And Pete said, "Hush."
>
> [William Faulkner, "Two Soldiers"]

Non-fiction:

> I located America thirty-one years ago in a Model-T Ford and planted my flag. I've tried a couple of times since to find it again, riding in faster cars and on better roads, but America is the sort of place that is discovered only once by any one man.
>
> [E. B. White, "From Sea to Shining Sea"]

Lead Length is Important

While a sparkling lead is critical, its length also is important. Today's lead must not be too short, nor too long, but like the temperature of Baby Bear's porridge, just right. The length is determined in part by your subject and the length of the story or article.

For example, if the editor only wants 1,200 words total, you cannot spend 500 on your introduction. It will have to be short and then get the readers right into the meat of the material.

In addition to word limits, some publications have their own particular style and preference for leads. Some may want short, snappy leads while others want slower paced ones. Lead length also can be affected by column width and size of type.

Examples of effective leads of different lengths:

On his bench in Madison Square, Soapy moved uneasily. When wild geese honk high of nights, and when women without sealskin coats grow kind to their husbands, and when Soapy moves uneasily on his bench in the park, you may know that winter is near at hand.

[O. Henry, "The Cop and the Anthem"]

An old man with steel-rimmed spectacles and very dusty clothes sat by the side of the road. There was a pontoon bridge across the river and carts, trucks, and men, women and children were crossing it. The mule-drawn carts staggered up the steep bank from the bridge with soldiers helping push against the spokes of the wheels. The trucks ground up and away heading out of it all and the peasants plodded along in the ankle-deep dust. But the old man sat there without moving. He was too tired to go any farther.

[Ernest Hemingway, "Old Man at the Bridge"]

About fifteen miles below Monterey, on the wild coast, the Torres family had their farm, a few sloping acres above a cliff that dropped to the brown reefs and to the hissing white waters of the ocean. Behind the farm the stone mountains stood up against the sky. The farm buildings huddled like the clinging aphids on the mountain skirts, crouched low to the ground as though the wind might blow them into the sea. The little shack, the rattling, rotting barn was gray-bitten with sea salt, beaten by the damp wind until they had taken on the color of the granite hills. Two horses, a red cow and a red calf, half a dozen pigs and a flock of lean multi-colored chickens stocked the place. A little corn was raised on the

sterile slope, and it grew short and thick under the wind, and all the
cobs formed on the landward sides of the stalks.

[John Steinbeck, "Flight"]

Good leads perform several functions. While we have been discussing them as attention-getters, they also can introduce the subject
and persuade the reader to stay with you. Remember, the readers'
primary interest is self, so try to give them a sense of participation
and involvement.

Chapter 5:

Mastering the Middle

You have worked diligently creating a great title and lead, now you can relax. WRONG! It *is* true you have hooked your readers, but unless you deliver what you promised, they are going to spit the hook out and go in search of more promising bait.

As you write the middle, it is important to pull your readers along from word to word, from sentence to sentence, from paragraph to paragraph, and from page to page. Some of your tools for this job, such as transitions, are discussed in other chapters.

Nonfiction Middles

As you write, put yourself in your readers' place. Ask yourself: If you were not familiar with the topic, would you understand the information given? Is it something you need or want to know? Is it presented in an interesting manner? Why should I take time out from my busy schedule to stop and read this?

Remember, you are writing for your readers, not yourself. Show them how your idea will make their lives better or easier. Use illustrations to make a point clearer. Use repetition and review to remind them of important points. As you continue into the body of the article, you may want to restate central themes where appropriate. And, of course, take your readers smoothly from one point to the next with proper transitions.

There are several methods you can use to write the middle. Sometimes you will use a combination of two or more in a single piece of writing. Your purpose for writing will determine which one(s) are most appropriate for your topic.

Process Method

If you are going to teach your readers how to do or make something, you will probably use the *process method*. You will explain how to bake a cake or install a new light fixture in a logical sequence. The process method also is useful when you want to explain how something works.

Chronological Method

The *chronological method* is similar to the process method. It gives events in the order they occurred. For example, if you are telling the story of your life you might start with when you were born, then on to your preschool and school days and up to the present time.

You do not need to give a complete detailed account of every event as that would become tedious and boring, except maybe to your mother. You would select events you think will interest your readers.

Descriptive Method

If you want to describe someone or something, use descriptive writing. Descriptive writing should appeal to as many of the five senses (sight, hearing, taste, touch, and smell) as possible. You create images in your readers' minds so they can see what you are describing.

A descriptive paragraph should focus on one person, object, place, or event. As you carefully select concrete and sensory details you will want to re-create the person or place for your readers. *Descriptive writing* details often are arranged in spatial order; that is, you choose a point, possibly the person's head, and work down to his feet, or vice versa.

Example:

"... that the stranger was neither Negro nor Indian. It is true he was dressed in a rude half-Indian garb and had a red belt or sash swathed round his body; but his face was neither black nor copper-color, but swarthy and dingy, and begrimed with soot, as if he had been accustomed to toil among fires and forges. He had a stock of coarse black hair, that stood out from his head in all directions, and bore an ax on his shoulder."

[From "The Devil and Tom Walker" by Washington Irving.]

Washington Irving does not describe the person's feet as he has not yet told his readers that this is the devil. If he had described the stranger's cloven feet it would have given it away.

Or, if you are describing a scene, you might start with details nearest you and move out to the horizon. The same is true when describing a place. If you are taking your readers on a tour of an ancient castle, you would not start in the dungeon under the castle because, unless you were on the starship Enterprise and beamed down, you could not have gotten there without walking through the rest of the castle first. So you would start in the courtyard, proceed into the castle, look around the various rooms, and then go down the dark, forbidding stairway to the dungeon.

Example:

> "Descending eastward, the highland meadows are a stairway to the plain. In July the inland slope of the Rockies is luxuriant with flax and buckeye, stonecrop and larkspur. The earth unfolds and the limit of the land recedes. Clusters of trees, and animals grazing far in the distance, cause the vision to reach away and wonder to build upon the mind. The sun follows a longer course in the day, and the sky is immense beyond all comparison. The great billowing clouds that sail upon it are shadows that move upon the grain like water, dividing light. Farther down, in the land of the Crows and Blackfeet, the plain is yellow. Sweet clover takes hold of the hills and bends upon itself to cover and seal the soil."

[N. Scott Momaday from *The Way to Rainy Mountain.*]

Comparison/Contrast

Comparison/contrast is useful when you are writing about two or more similar things. Comparison shows their similarities; contrast, their differences. One technique presents the information in an alternating AB AB AB way. As each point about one item is completed, it is followed with a similar point about the other.

Example AB AB AB:

> At first glance, the undersea world of the scuba diver appears quite different than the outer space world of the astronaut. However, they are not as different as one might think. For example, a scuba diver wears a wet suit for protection from the cold water. In like manner, an astronaut wears a space suit to protect him from

heat and radiation. The scuba diver uses air tanks to breathe under water and the astronaut uses the oxygen systems of his spacecraft or suit to breathe in outer space. Each explores worlds normally not visited by man. The scuba diver explores the oceans in search of adventure and for a closer look at marine life. The astronaut explores outer space for adventure and a closer look at our neighboring planets. Finally, the scuba diver's return to the surface must be slow to avoid dangerous rapid pressure changes. Likewise, the astronaut must make his return to earth protected from reentry heat by special tile heat shields.

A second method is to present all the details about one are presented before discussing the second item AAA BBB.

Example AAA BBB:

At first glance, the undersea world of the scuba diver appears quite different than the outer space world of the astronaut. However, they are not as different as you might think. A scuba diver wears a wet suit for protection from the cold water. In addition, the scuba diver explores the oceans in search of adventure and for a closer look at marine life. Finally, the scuba diver's return to the surface must be slow to avoid dangerous rapid pressure changes. While exploring outer space, an astronaut wears a space suit to protect him from heat and radiation. And, the astronaut explores outer space for adventure and a closer look at our neighboring planets. The astronaut must make his return to earth protected from reentry heat by special tile heat shields. Thus, each explores worlds normally not visited by man. As you can see, the worlds of the scuba diver and the astronaut are not as different as one might think.

Whichever pattern you choose, be sure your handling is balanced. Every point of the comparison or contrast must be applied to both items. For example, if you were comparing or contrasting the styles of two basketball players and you discussed one's unique freethrow shooting style, you also must discuss the other's freethrow style.

Comparison and contrast can be used separately or together to develop an idea or relate two or more things. The most effective comparisons show similarities between ideas or things usually regarded as different, e.g., the flow of water and the flow of electric current. Likewise, the most effective contrasts result from contrasting ideas or things that are usually regarded as similar, e.g., the habits of dogs and wolves.

Examples:

Comparison:

> In some ways the flow of water is similar to the flow of electricity. For example, while water is carried by pipes, electricity is carried by wires. In addition, a faucet controls the flow of water and a switch controls the flow of electric current. And, just as water pressure can vary, so can electricity. So, while water and electricity are different in many ways, the way they get to us has several similarities.

Contrast:

> Although they appear quite similar, in many ways wolves are unlike dogs. For instance, all wolves are basically the same size, while dogs vary in size from the tiny Chihuahua to the giant Bull Mastiff. In addition, wolves travel in packs, while dogs most often travel alone. Their eating habits are quite different as well. Wolves eat whatever they can kill, while dogs eat whatever their masters put in their dishes. So, while wolves and dogs are closely related, there are still many differences between them.

In Analogy

Comparison/contrast also can join elements in different classes. This type of comparison is called *analogy,* and is useful when we need to explain or illuminate an unfamiliar, complex, abstract class of things with a familiar and concrete class of things. For example, suppose you wanted someone unfamiliar with the operation of a computer to understand how information is stored and retrieved. By using an analogy, you could compare the storage area on a disk with a file cabinet drawer full of file folders. A person unfamiliar with a computer would then understand how the storage system works.

Arthur M. Kassel used analogy to explain how drugs affect the brain and shut down its production of Endorphins. They are the body's natural narcotic and are released in times of mental stress or physical pain:

> To put it in simple terms, everyone has a thyroid gland, and if you take three grains of thyroid a day for three to six months, you shut off your body's own ability to make thyroid. If you ever stop taking those grains of thyroid, you may find that your thyroid will never regenerate to the extent that your body will make its own natural substance. There is unequivocal evidence in animals and indirect evidence in humans which reveals that when you take external heroin, morphine, methadone, codeine, darvon, or any other narcotic, you shut down the brain's ability to make endorphins. The experts have taken blood samples from heroin and methadone addicts, and they have been able to show a diminution in these addicts' endorphins.

A word of caution: Sometimes an analogy is offered as proof of an idea. It should not be used this way. An analogy does not prove, it only helps explain a concept.

Cause and Effect

Another useful organizational method is *cause and effect*. You can use this method in one of two ways. You can start with the causes that produce an effect, or start with the effect that the causes produce. Your purpose for writing will determine your approach.

If your purpose is to demonstrate why something exists or occurs, then the effects-to-causes approach is your better choice. On the other hand, if your purpose is to demonstrate the consequences, then the causes-to-effects order better suits your purpose. Cause and effect is especially useful when you want to write about social, economic, or political events or problems.

Example, cause to effects:

> The shrinking in size of the microchip and the explosion of computer technology has caused a resolution of sorts in today's society. The fax machine allows businesses to transmit information across the street or around the world in a matter of minutes. Also, instead of records being kept in bulky files, business information now can be stored compactly on disks and is available almost instantly at the stroke of a computer key. In addition, databases accessible with computer modems have made research, travel arrangements, and even shopping available to anyone with a computer and modem. And she doesn't have to leave home or office. The microchip has truly revolutionized the world we live in.

Example, effects to cause:

> In the large city, the buildings have a gray dingy appearance. The sky changes from a brilliant blue to a hazy grey-blue hue. At night, few stars are visible in the charcoal grey sky, and they do not twinkle like they do in the country. Cars and bridges rust and building surfaces erode. People prone to lung problems spend more time in bed sick. Is it possible for one thing to cause all this? Unfortunately, it is. Air pollution is a price we seem forced to pay for progress.

A word of caution: Be sure one event or condition is actually the cause of another. Just because one occurred or existed before the other does not mean they have a cause and effect relationship. For example, you could not say that Harvey causes it to rain just because every time you invite him over for a cookout it rains. Likewise, you could not say that all crime is the result of poverty. Obviously, all poor people are not criminals and all criminals are not poor. Poverty may be a contributing factor in some crime but does not cause all of it.

Order of Importance

Another organizational method is **order of importance.** In this method, you assign a degree of value, power, authority, interest, or quality to each item you wish to discuss. While you can go from most important to least important to arouse interest at the beginning, this order runs the risk of your readers forgetting how important the first item is when they get to the end. Personally, I prefer to start with the least important and build to a crescendo at the end. This sends readers away saying, "Wow! That really is important!"

Example, least to most:

A policeman needs certain qualities to gain the respect of those he serves. It is important for him to treat people graciously and politely. In addition, he should not lose self-control in an emergency, but remain in control of his emotions and the situation. It is extremely important that he has a complete understanding of the law and of citizen's rights. Most important of all, he must enforce the law fairly. Like justice, he needs to be blind and treat everyone equally. If he possesses these vital attributes, he will be successful in his chosen profession.

Order of Generality

In the *order of generality* method, you arrange your ideas according to their breadth or scope. To go from the general to the specific, start by presenting your most general idea or ideas and then work through them in a stairstep fashion to the most specific point. Or reverse the order and start with a very specific item and work up to your most general statement.

Picture a pyramid in your mind. Think about each of your ideas. A general idea goes at the base. A more specific idea goes in the middle. And if it is very specific, it goes at the very top. To go from general to specific, you invert the pyramid and present the most general, broadest, idea first and work down to the most specific, most narrow, idea. Leave the pyramid right side up for the most specific to general presentation.

This method can be useful in persuasive writing. You can first present an overview of the problem, then provide specific concrete evidence for each point along the way.

Example, general to specific:

> A major concern facing our nation's youth today is a general lack of physical fitness. Today's young people are more often spectators than participants in sports activities. Playing sports offers young people one way to become physically fit. They should pick a sport they enjoy, such as swimming, and participate in it often. Swimming is one of the few physical activities that offers a total body workout. Since most young people enjoy a day at the beach or pool with their friends, planning a swimming outing is a good way to encourage physical fitness.

Personal Experience

Another popular type of nonfiction writing is the *personal experience* essay. In it, you tell something that happened to you that you feel will help others. Many magazines print personal experiences and some, such as *Guideposts,* are almost exclusively personal experience essays.

Your purpose may be to inform, entertain, or inspire your readers. Whatever it is, you will be telling a true story and communicating your feelings and reactions in vivid word pictures. You will retell a significant, true experience and present the sequence of details in an unaffected and clear tone.

You will want to use a narrative and probably chronological style to tell your story. You also will want to include as many specific, concrete details as possible. There may be places you will want to foreshadow upcoming events or flashback to previous ones.

The ending should provide a "take-away" for your readers. "She made it. I can, too."

Your tone can vary from humorous to somber, depending on the topic. Since you are relating a personal experience, you will want to write it in first person.

Categories Method

You may find, however, that what you are planning to write really doesn't fit any of the methods already discussed. Then, you may need to use the *categories method,* the most flexible method of all. In it you take all the information you have collected and divide it into groups, or categories. The job of division will be easier if your information is on 3 x 5 cards that you can stack in neat piles.

Let's say you are going to write about ways high school seniors can raise money for a special project. You find you have the following seven ideas:

1. Sell candy.

2. Run the concessions stand at a ball game.

3. Ask class members to contribute money.

4. Collect paper, aluminum, and glass for recycling.

5. Have a car wash.

6. Have a walk-a-thon and get pledges from sponsors.

7. Sponsor an after-game dance.

Now it's time to think about what order to present the suggestions to your readers. Unlike the process and chronological methods, there is not a right and wrong order. However, the categories method does offer both good and better ways. Just as you want to put your most important or interesting information at the beginning and end of a paragraph, you want to grab your readers with high interest ideas and leave them with high interest ones as well. Put the ones you feel they will be least enthusiastic about in the middle. Thus, you might start with number seven, sponsoring a dance, and end with number six, having a walk-a-thon, because both probably will generate a lot of enthusiasm among the students. Since number three, asking them for donations, will not be a favorite, it should be in the middle of the list.

As you put your ideas into categories think about different approaches you can take with the subject. Your approach determines what some of the categories will be and how you will put the article together. Your choice will, in part, be determined by your purpose, your knowledge of your audience, and your writing style.

Persuasive Writing

Different types of articles need different approaches. For example, if you are writing a *persuasive article* you should feel strongly about your topic. Thus, you will have a strong point of view. However, it is important to let your readers know that you are aware of other sides to the issue. If you don't, your readers are likely to reject your arguments as being completely biased.

You will, however, want to devote eighty-five to ninety percent of your space to your own side, and present the opposition in as few sentences as possible without appearing to be unfair. It also is important to arrange your arguments carefully. If you present your strongest ones first and then work down to your weakest, your readers will go away feeling it isn't so important after all and you have lost the argument. Readers tend to remember longest the last thing they read, so save your best and strongest arguments for last.

Anecdotes

Anecdotes are important ingredients in nonfiction writing. Everyone loves a story. What better way to reinforce a point than with an illustration from life?

Anecdotes can sum up ideas. They also can help readers see your point more clearly. They can elicit a desired emotional response from them, making them laugh or cry. They can give a glimpse into the unfamiliar or let readers imagine what could be or might have been.

Here are some ways to spot places in your writing that can use anecdotes:

1. If the section seems to be just plodding along dully, it's time for a story.

2. If you have presented complex ideas an anecdote can sum up and illustrate them. It gives your readers an image that helps solidify your statements. Or it simply can amuse or distract them for a moment before continuing on with the business at hand.

However, be certain the anecdote has a reason to be there. Putting one in that has no connection with the point defeats its purpose. The unconnected anecdote will jar your readers and they will have to stop and try to figure out why you included it. Before adding an anecdote, ask yourself:

1. Does the anecdote help prove my point?

2. Is it related to the point or does it wander off on its own?

3. If it is a true story, do I say it is? An anecdote can be fictional, but be sure you tell the readers it is.

4. Will it evoke strong emotions in the readers? Are they the emotions I want them to experience?

5. Have I, either at the beginning or end of the anecdote, clearly shown how it proves my point?

Logical Order

As you write, be sure to present the information in a *logical order*. For example, if you are giving your readers a step-by-step process for making a pumpkin pie, you would not have them pour the pumpkin into the pie crust and then add the spices. That would be illogical. Or if you are giving the steps for changing a flat tire, you would not have them remove the flat tire before jacking the car up.

A description of a person, place, or thing needs to be in logical spatial order. You would not start by describing the blouse or shirt a person was wearing, then move to the shoes, then up to the hat and finally describe the skirt or slacks. The reader would be totally confused because these present no logical sequence. You want to find a logical starting point and begin there. When describing a person, for example, start with the feet or head and work up or down as the case might be.

Symbols in Writing

Symbols are all around us. Some, like our flag, are so familiar we take them for granted. Fables have taught us that the fox is *sly,* the owl is *wise,* and the mule and ox are *stubborn.* Christian baptism is a symbol of faith in Christ; the wedding ring a symbol of undying love. Throughout the centuries, outstanding writers have used symbols to help achieve a greater depth in their writing and more subtle levels of meaning.

Colors can hold symbolic significance for us. Black cats, black clouds, and black veils all give us a sense of foreboding and an expectation of bad things to come. On the other hand, white symbolizes life and purity and gives us a sense of well-being and good things to come.

In his short story, "The Masque of the Red Death," Edgar Allen Poe uses red to set the tone of pain and agony:

> The "*Red* Death" had long devastated the country. No pestilence had ever been so fatal or so hideous. *Blood* was its Avatar and its seal—the *redness* and the horror of *blood*. There were sharp pains, and sudden dizziness, and then profuse *bleeding* at the pores, with dissolution. The *scarlet* stains upon the body and especially upon the face of the victim were the pest ban which shut him out from the aid and from the sympathy of his fellowmen. And the whole seizure, progress, and termination of the disease were the incidents of half an hour.

Later in the story, Poe uses colors, in addition to an east to west arrangement of the rooms, to symbolize birth to death:

> ...These windows were of stained glass whose color varied in accordance with the prevailing hue of the decorations of the chamber into which it opened. That at the eastern extremity was hung, for example, in *blue*—and vividly blue were its windows. The second chamber was *purple* in its ornaments and tapestries, ...The third was *green* throughout, ...The fourth was furnished and lighted with *orange*—the fifth with *white*—the sixth with *violet*. The seventh apartment was closely shrouded in *black* velvet tapestries...But in this chamber only, the color of the windows failed to correspond with the decorations. The panes here were *scarlet*—a deep *blood* color.

Some psychologists have affiliated symbolic subconscious messages with particular colors. They generally correlate them as follows:

Black—death

White—life; purity

Grey—elements of life and death

Red—pain; bloodshed; agony; danger

Green—rebirth; freshness

Brown—of the earth

Purple—royalty; elegance; power

Pink—femininity

Gold—wealth

Yellow—blindness (negative) or enlightenment (positive)

Other Considerations

Unless what they are reading is something very technical, readers often tend to skim as they read. Therefore, whether you are writing fiction or nonfiction, you should put the most important information at the beginning and end of each paragraph. That's not to say you can put any old thing in the middle, you just put the most important where it is easy to find.

Now that you have the middle of your article or story in good shape, it is time to put an unforgettable ending on it. For more help in writing fiction middles, see chapter 8, "Fabricating Fabulous Fiction."

Chapter 6:

Don't Leave Them Hanging

Sometimes a mountain climber loses his footing and finds himself dangling at the end of his safety rope. Not a pleasant place to be. Fortunately for him, his climbing partners will not leave him hanging but will pull him back to safety.

We writers sometimes leave our readers hanging when we do not put a satisfactory conclusion on our articles or stories. This leaves readers dangling in mid-air looking for a way to get safely down to earth. To keep from leaving readers dangling, it is necessary to finish each article or story with an appropriate ending.

NONFICTION

Just as there are several different types of articles, there are several different ways to end them. The type of ending you choose will depend on the type of article you have written.

Informative Articles

If an article basically gives information, the conclusion may simply go back and restate the introduction. It should, however, incorporate a broader perspective, including some reference to material in the body of the article.

Example:

> An article about dogs as pets might begin: "Almost as many breeds of dogs exist as different types of people who own them."

It might end with:

> "As you can see, why people want a pet and where they live also affects which breed of dog they choose."

This ending has not only gone back to the beginning, but also has referred briefly to some information in the article. Coming full circle leaves a satisfactory conclusion.

Solution Endings

If the purpose of the article is to discuss a problem, then the ending should suggest a solution. In fact, it may include steps readers can take to solve it.

For example, the problem may be what to do with a houseful of active children on a rainy day. Obviously, a problem that needs a solution. A summary of the ideas in the article could be used as the conclusion:

> So, to keep the children from just sitting in front of the television or destroying the house, try these ideas:

1. Have them shape animals out of molding clay.

2. Have them make cards out of construction paper to send to someone who is ill or lonely.

3. Have them make hand puppets and act out a favorite story.

4. Have a baking day and help them make roll-out cookies. They can cut and decorate them.

Now, armed with these ideas, you will not have to panic the next time rain is forecast.

This summary ending gives readers a quick review and a handy reference of the main ideas.

How-to or Process Articles

A similar type of article is the how-to. However, instead of suggestions to solve the problem, the how-to could be ended with a restating of the steps involved in the process.

Example:

Now you won't have to panic the next time it's your turn to entertain the tribe, if you follow this time schedule for organizing your holiday preparations:

The first week in November: Mark all special dates for the season on your calendar. Start collecting stocking- stuffers. Plan your Thanksgiving dinner menu. Gather your favorite recipes together. Make a list of ingredients for Thanksgiving and Christmas baking. Buy everything now.

The second week in November: Order catalog gifts. Buy Christmas turkey, if you have extra freezer space available. Check your cooking utensils and serving dishes, et cetera, to see if any need replacing. Shop for nonperishable food items for Thanksgiving. Check to be sure all electrical appliances are in working order. Decide what holiday decorations you are going to make.

The third week in November: Do some gift shopping. Polish silver. Make edible gifts. Buy Christmas cards—and stamps.

The fourth week in November: Send invitations out for holiday parties. Plan holiday menus. Make fruitcakes. Make and freeze hors d'oeuvres and casseroles.

Two days before Thanksgiving and other holidays: Buy perishables. Trim vegetables and store in plastic bags in the refrigerator.

One day before: Bake pies. Wash and dry salad ingredients; refrigerate. Set table. Assemble serving dishes and utensils in kitchen. Prepare stuffing ingredients; store dry and liquid ingredients separately in refrigerator.

The day: Note specific times to do each food preparation. Relax and enjoy yourself.

You will find that by planning ahead, you have taken the hassle out of holiday planning and everyone will have a much more enjoyable time.

Personal Experience

The personal experience article requires yet another type of conclusion. Here it is appropriate to end with a personal reaction to or observation about the experience. It even could be a lesson learned.

The article might be about a first visit to the Statue of Liberty. In the article the writer has told about the trip and what actually seeing Miss Liberty for the first time meant to her.

Example:

While I was born in the United States, I couldn't help thinking back to my immigrant ancestors and how they must have felt when they finally sailed close enough to America to see her. I am truly grateful that they made that difficult trip so I could be born and raised in this great nation.

Descriptive Writing

A description of a scene simply may bring the reader back to the starting point.

Example:

> The view from the veranda was breathtaking. Just below was an immaculately kept garden with many varieties of exotic tropical plants. Here and there, tiny birds darted from flower to flower. Straight ahead, past the garden wall, the sun cast its golden rays over the Pacific Ocean. To my left, near the horizon, a sailboat added to the beauty of the scene, while on the right children laughed and played on the beach. I wished the scene could last forever. However, darkness soon settled on the scene as though someone had dropped a heavy blanket over the only light in the room.

Notice how the description started near the veranda, and as it ended the scene is being covered by darkness.

Persuasive Writing

A well-written persuasive article should have readers ready to go out and do something. It can end with some suggested action. An article about air pollution and what can be done to improve air quality could be ended:

If you are concerned about the quality of the air we breathe, here is how you can make a difference:

1. Be sure your car is properly tuned up.

2. Don't buy products known to pollute the atmosphere.

3. Work to get clean air legislation passed in your town, county, and state.

4. Support groups fighting to clean up our air.

5. Ask those running for public office about their stand on clean air. By taking action, you can breathe easier and so can your family and friends.

Include Something New

Yet another way to end an article is with a point or idea not covered in the article, but closely related to the rest of it. For example, an article about different ways to beautify a yard could be ended:

> "For that finishing touch of color, plant a variety of perennials along the walks."

Revising the End

As you revise, check to see that you have kept your purpose clearly in focus throughout the article because purpose will affect your conclusion. In addition, keep your readers in mind and give them what you promised at the beginning.

Be sure you have not left your readers hanging in midair. A good way to check the ending is to ask someone else to read your article to see if it has a satisfactory conclusion. While you may think everything has been said that needs to be, another person may think something is missing.

Remember, the type of article you have written will determine the type of ending needed:

1. An informational article ending can restate the introduction and add a little information.

2. The problem-solving article conclusion can suggest solutions. Or it can end with a final point not covered in the body of the article.

3. Likewise, a how-to article may end with a restatement of the steps involved or the main points covered.

4. A personal comment may be used as the conclusion to a personal experience article.

5. A description may bring readers back to the starting point.

6. A persuasive article may conclude with some action for readers to take.

Some Nonfiction Ending Techniques

1. *Recap.* As you reread your lead, write an ending that answers the problems you raised for your readers or completely proves points you made earlier.

2. *Give your article an unexpected ending.* Add an outlandish or ironic, yet logical, twist ending. For example: After spending thirty years working in a sewing factory sweatshop, Alice retires and goes into business for herself—sewing and alterations.

3. *Use a forceful quotation.* The quotation may be from an authority you featured in the article, or someone else who has something memorable to say about your subject. In an article I wrote on drunk driving, I quoted Don "Big Daddy" Garlits, a top drag race driver. He had participated in a "Drunk Driver's Rodeo" sponsored by the Florida Junior Chamber of Commerce and had stated after the rodeo: "I've come to the conclusion that you shouldn't drive even if you have had only one drink. That's a pretty strong statement, but I think it's the only answer."

4. *Use a joke or pun.* Almost everyone enjoys a good laugh. So, if you can, leave them smiling. You've probably already left them with a thought. The joke or pun can be used to summarize and provide entertainment. Be judicious in using humor because some subjects simply are not funny.

5. *Confirm what you stated in the article.* You present disturbing, yet conclusive, facts that clearly restate your position and allow your readers to leave agreeing with you.

FICTION

Fiction, like nonfiction, needs a proper ending. Mickey Spillane has said, "The first chapter sells the book, the last chapter sells the *next* book."

The ending is a sales pitch for what you have just read, as well as the author's next book. If you like a book you will tell your friends about it. If you have ever read a story that didn't end satisfactorily, you felt unfulfilled, cheated, and maybe a little angry. When Charles Dickens originally published *Great Expectations,* he ended it with Pip and Estella meeting after many years and then going their separate ways. His readers did not like that ending and raised such a clamor that Dickens had to rewrite the ending with Pip and Estella finally getting together permanently.

The ending must deliver what the story or book has promised. All loose ends need to be tied up. This does not mean you cannot leave it open for a sequel, but the conflicts in that story should be resolved. To be sure you have done this, you may want to chart the story as you go. Note additions of characters and plot twists and make sure they are all resolved in the end.

Dennis E. Hensley tells of bringing in a minor character for a few scenes in one of the Leslie Holden novels he co-authored with Holly G. Miller. He then had the character leave the action because he felt she was too minor to bother about again. However, his editors had a strong desire to know whatever had happened to that character; Hensley ultimately had to rewrite several chapters to bring that character back into the story in order to resolve the action involving her.

Like Hensley, you may feel everything is taken care of, but someone else might not. Therefore, it is a good idea to have someone, or several people, if possible, read your story or book expressly to see if you have tied up all the loose ends. Often, you are too close to the story and have the plot in your head, yet you may have failed to put it on paper.

I once had a student who was an excellent fiction writer. One day she gave me a story that had a plot switch in the middle. On paper she had failed to move the action from one situation to the next. However, when I asked her about it, she was able to tell me the connection as she had conceived it in her head. She simply had neglected to write it down.

Alas, your readers will not have the opportunity to ask you about something that may confuse them. So you need to be sure all their questions are answered on paper.

Tying Up Loose Ends

As with nonfiction, there are several ways to put a satisfactory ending on your fictional story. If it is a short story with a basic story line and no subplots, you may simply satisfactorily solve the problem that you presented at the beginning and tie up any loose ends.

Saki does this in his short story "The Cobweb."

Beginning:

The farmhouse kitchen probably stood where it did as a matter of accident or haphazard choice; yet its situation might have been planned by a master-strategist in farmhouse architecture. Dairy and poultry-yard, and herb garden, and all the busy places of the farm seemed to lead by easy access into its wide flagged haven, where there was room for everything and where muddy boots left traces that were easily swept away. And yet, for all that it stood so well in the center of human bustle, its long, latticed window, with the wide window-seat, built into an embrasure beyond the huge fireplace, looked out on a wild spreading view of hill and heather and wooded combe. The window nook made almost a little room in itself, quite the pleasantest room in the farm as far as situation and capabilities went. Young Mrs. Ladbruk, whose husband had just come into the farm by way of inheritance, cast covetous eyes on this snug corner, and her fingers itched to make it bright and cozy with chintz curtains and bowls of flowers, and a shelf or two of old china. The musty farm parlour, looking out to a prim, cheerless garden imprisoned within high, blank walls, was not a room that lent itself readily either to comfort or decoration.

Last paragraph:

The farm was a family property, and passed to the rabbit-shooting cousin as the next-of-kin. Emma Ladbruk drifted out of its history as a bee that had wandered in at an open window might flit its way out again. On a cold grey morning she stood waiting with her boxes already stowed in the farm cart, till the last of the market produce should be ready, for the train she was to catch was of less importance than the chickens and butter and eggs that were to be offered for sale. From where she stood she could see the angle of the long latticed window that was to have been cozy with curtains and gay with bowls of flowers. Into her mind came the thought that for months, perhaps for years, long after she had been utterly forgotten, a white, unheeding face would be seen peering out through those latticed panes, and a weak muttering voice would be heard quavering up and down those flagged passages. She made her way to a narrow barred casement that opened into the farm larder. Old Martha was standing at a table trussing a pair of chickens for the market stall as she had trussed them for nearly fourscore years.

The Ironic Twist

You may have led your readers to believe things were going to end one way and then give the story an *ironic twist* so it does not end as expected. Be sure, however, the ending is a logical one or your readers will feel they have been had.

Each week *Woman's World* magazine has a feature called "Mini Mystery." This is a one-page mystery on the last page of the magazine and is the first thing I read because I know it will be exciting and have a surprise ending.

Example:

> Harry's wife, Edith was a compulsive gambler and was rapidly sending them to the poor house. He planned to kill her and collect on her life insurance policy so he could start living. Meanwhile she won the lottery and a chance to spin a wheel on television for up to $10 million. To win, the ball had to stay in the slot in front of the amount for three seconds. She spun the wheel and the ball fell in the $10 million slot only to bounce out and into the $1,000 one. Back in their hotel room, Harry pushed Edith off the balcony, satisfied it would look like an accident and he would be able to collect double indemnity on her insurance policy. Almost immediately the telephone rang and one of the judges told Harry that after reviewing the tape they decided the ball had stayed in the $10 million slot the necessary three seconds—but only Mrs. Johnson could claim the prize money.
>
> ["Jackpot!" by Helen Voller, Woman's World, May 22, 1990, p. 54.]

Mystery stories, however, are not the only kind that can have an ironic twist to them. An example is the short story, "The Verger," by Somerset Maugham. The verger is a caretaker of the interior of a church. Albert Edward Foreman lost his job as verger because he could not read and write, which had nothing to do with the job. The new vicar just felt it "wasn't proper" to have a verger who was illiterate. After being fired, Albert opened a series of very successful shops and made a fortune. Years later when his banker learned that Albert could not read or write he was almost speechless:

> "And do you mean to say that you've built up this important business and amassed a fortune of thirty thousand pounds without being able to read or write? Good God, man, what would you be now if you had been able to?"
>
> "I can tell you that, sir," said Mr. Foreman, a little smile on his still aristocratic features. "I'd be verger of St. Peter's, Neville Square."

Know Where You Are Going

You should be working toward your ending throughout your writing, otherwise it can be tacked on and weak. While you won't always know the end before you start writing, if possible write the last paragraph before you start. This will give you a destination to strive to reach as you write. While all roads lead to Rome, you are still in Rome when you get there.

It's like driving at night. If you know your destination even though you cannot see past the beam of your headlights, you will still get there because you know where you are going. Likewise, if you have your ending planned ahead of time, no matter how many detours you take along the way, you eventually will reach your Rome.

Mystery writer Dorothy Salisbury Davis says that she can't comfortably write a mystery novel unless she knows who did it when she starts writing. Now, she may change her mind along the way and end up with a different killer, but she always has a solution in mind as she fabricates the plot.

Satisfactory Endings

1. To satisfy your readers your ending should be a logical consequence of the events in the story.

2. Your ending must not depend on coincidence. This makes a very weak ending. Your readers will feel you couldn't come up with a logical ending, so you made one up. Unfortunately, they probably are right.

3. Your ending cannot be predictable. While an ending must be logical, the readers should not go away thinking they knew all along how it would end.

4. If possible, have the resolution of a mystery use the "Ball of Twine" technique. In this technique, you first solve the last mystery presented, then work your way back to the beginning. The Ball of Twine can be used in most types of fiction and is not limited to mystery writing.

5. Any symbolism you have used should be clear. Symbols can add emotional impact throughout the story, but they are particularly significant at the end.

6. The ending should complete the story. Don't leave your reader hanging in the air looking for a way down.

7. The ending should be just the right length. Not too short to tie all the loose ends together, and not so long that it loses its effectiveness. Don't try to extend too far into your protagonist's future. Just point the characters in the right direction and let them go on their way by themselves. Besides, this can give you an opening for a sequel.

Why Endings Fail

1. They are unresolved. The writer is finished, but the action isn't. Often beginning writers run out of something to say so they just stop. They don't take into consideration that without a proper ending they have left their readers dangling. Readers want to be safely on the ground when they finish reading.

2. The ending is redundant. The writer has simply rehashed what was already written and not said anything new. This is not the same as coming full circle.

3. It is listless. Rather than coming to a definite conclusion, it drifts off into the sunset. It's about as exciting as driving your car, seeing a stop sign half a block ahead, taking your foot off the gas

pedal, and gradually coasting to a stop. Boring. Miller Williams says that after reading the last line of one of his poems he wants his readers to "go through the windshield."

4. It is one-sided. While good persuasive writing is intended to change readers' opinions, the ending should give the readers credit for enough brains to figure it out for themselves. It should *not* tell them what they should be thinking.

5. It is unrelated to the rest of the article or story. Near the end, the writer takes off on an unrelated tangent and ends there, never returning to the main point.

Keep your ending in mind throughout the entire writing process. As you write nonfiction, jot down ideas, one-liners, exciting facts, or terrific anecdotes that you can use for an ending.

For fiction, have your story ending in mind so you will have a destination to travel to. Be sure it is a logical, although not predictable conclusion. It must fit the story and tell enough, but not too much. It should be decisive, not slowly drifting off to nowhere.

Now, with a proper ending, your readers will not be left dangling in mid-air, but will be safely back on the ground when they finish reading.

To end this chapter, I leave you with a quotation from Shakespeare: "All's well that ends well."

Chapter 7:

The Title's The Thing

A rose by any other name may smell as sweet, but will a book, article, or story without a great title sell as well? The title gives readers their first impression of what you've written. The title must give them a reason to want to at least look at it. Recently while searching for intriguing titles, I came across an article entitled "Are You a Skid-Talker?" I had to stop and read it because the author, Corey Ford, had aroused my curiosity. It was about people, mostly his wife, who put two thoughts that don't make sense together, for example, "Two can live as cheaply as one, but it costs twice as much." Had he titled it "Silly Things My Wife Says," I doubt I would have stopped to read it. However, by coining a new word and using it to ask a question, he hooked me. If readers don't pick up your book or stop to read your article or story in the magazine you have lost them before they start.

A title needs to indicate what's coming, but not give away the plot. For example, I'm presently writing a humor piece about my "brown thumb"—as opposed to some people's "green thumbs." My working title is "Plant's Lament." However, I know that won't be the final one because at the beginning I don't want the readers to know I'm talking about plants. Nor would *The Butler Did It* be a good choice for the title of a murder mystery as the suspense would be gone. Nobody wants to read a mystery when they already know who did it.

A ho-hum title also can keep a manuscript from getting past the editor's desk. Editors are busy people and you must grab their attention immediately. Titles can help do that. What if Peter Benchley had called his book *The Adventures of Sheriff Martin Brody* instead of *Jaws*? What's there to interest readers?

However, don't stop writing because you don't have a block-buster title thought up. Final titles often don't come until after much thought and anguish. Just get a working title and start writing.

Know Your Audience

Just as it is important to know your audience when writing your article or story, you must keep them in mind when you choose a title. Be sure it will have meaning for them. For example, if you are explaining fundamental principles of computer operation to a general audience, you would not use computer jargon in your title. They would not understand it. You would want something like "Unraveling the Mystery of Computers" or "Computer Basics for Beginners." However, if your audience has a good working knowledge of computers you could use one like "Managing DOS on Your Hard Disk" because they will understand it.

It also is important to give your readers what you have promised in the title. For instance, if your title promises "10 Economical Ways to Keep Cool Next Summer," you would not give them eight or even twelve. And you would not include ideas that were going to cost a lot of money, because you promised the ideas would be affordable for most readers. Otherwise they will feel cheated.

Clever Title Ideas

Use *alliteration*. In alliteration, each word starts with the same sound, usually a consonant, like "Tremendous Tommy" or "Battling Bongos." When I wrote an article on marijuana for the teen market I wanted to use alliteration to create a memorable title while conveying the idea that marijuana causes problems. Since a slang name for marijuana is "weed," I decided to use that, but needed something to go with it. Back to my faithful thesaurus I went and found "wily," which means "a trick or stratagem intended to ensnare or deceive." There was my title: "The Wily Weed." It tells the readers what to expect and is an intriguing way for them to remember it. A *Saturday Evening Post* article about Katherine Hepburn was titled: "Courageous, Cantankerous, Candid Kate."

Or you can *contrast* someone or something in a unique and unexpected way: "Steve Martin: Wild and Serious Guy," or "The Warmhearted Polar Bear."

A *well-known quotation* can give you an unforgettable title. You can use it as is or give it a new twist as Erma Bombeck did for her best-selling book *Family, The Ties That Bind...And Gag.* Other titles with a twist: "Amazing Gracie," "Long Time, No Ski," and "Road's Scholar."

How-to titles are always popular. Look at the nonfiction books in any bookstore and see how many titles start with "how-to." We want to know how to do better whatever we're interested in. The same is true for magazine articles. Count the number of how-to articles in them. Maybe how-to isn't in the title, but the message is there: "Fifty Ways to Brighten Your Day" or "Ten Guaranteed Ways to Get That Raise." People are interested in how you can make their lives better or easier. They want to know what you can do for them.

In fact, the 1988 writers' guidelines for *Cosmopolitan* magazine state: "All nonfiction should tell their readers how they can improve their lives, better enjoy their lives, and live better lives."

Or you might submit a **question** to your readers that they want answered: "Are You Afraid to be Happy?" "Is Your Home Safe for Pets?" "How Safe Is Our Blood Supply?"

A **rhyming** title also can catch your readers' attention: "Vets on Pets" or "Putting the Pedal to your Mettle."

Poems, nursery rhymes, songs, Shakespeare and the Bible are all good sources of titles. They can be used as is or given an attention-grabbing twist.

Examples:

"To Sleep, Perchance—," "Disney World and the Four Dwarfs," "Lead Us Not into McDonald's," "And the Van Played On," "The Fairest of Them All," and "Deck Your Halls with Houseplants."

Titles with a Twist

You can take a familiar title and give it a twist creating a title readers will remember: "The Great Termite Race," "My Contractor,

My Self," "New Mexico's 'Mission Possible.'" While titles cannot be copyrighted, it is not a good idea to lift them verbatim. Not only can this cause confusion, but it shows a lack of creativity.

Creating a Title

Your manuscript is finished, but you still don't have an attention-grabbing title. What do you do? Just as when revising the manuscript, you may need to put it away for a few days to cool so you can take a fresher look at title possibilities. You may need to reread it several times.

Key phrases or ideas also can be used as a title. Look for short, to-the-point questions or sentences that seem to sparkle and jump off the page as you read them. An article I wrote on smoking ended up being titled "Half Cup of Tar a Year" because that is how much the average pack-a-day smokers deposit in their lungs each year.

If you're fortunate enough to have a friend or family member who will read your manuscript and offer helpful suggestions, you might ask for help in brainstorming. Or just sit down yourself and write down every title possibility you can. Don't worry about them being good or even making sense. When you get through there just may be a germ there that will send you on your way to a gem of a title.

A good exercise to stimulate your creative title juices is to think up new and clever titles for articles or stories you have read. See if you can come up with a new slant or idea that is better than the one the author used.

As a general rule, limit title lengths to six words or less. However, as with most writing rules, you can have successful exceptions.

Even after you have decided on a title, go back from time to time and take a hard look at the titles of articles or stories that haven't sold after several trips to editors. Just maybe a fresh title will help. In fact, as you submit to different markets, study each magazine to see what kind of titles they use most. Some use the verb, action style of a newspaper, while others are precise and matter-of-fact. Some feature intriguing headlines. Remember the titles on the cover are often what sell the magazine, especially while you're standing in line at the checkout counter. Some editors want a subtitle as well as a title. So, as you go from market to market, you need to be aware of their style and needs.

Try to think up several titles for your article or story. You even may want to attach some of the more creative ones in a postscript to your manuscript so the editor can choose a different one, if he prefers. While editors often change titles to suit their own needs, that doesn't mean you should not come up with the best title you possibly can. Remember, you've got to grab the editor's attention first.

Keep any title ideas you may have. You never know when you will want to use a different one or when one you have thought up for one piece of writing will work on another.

Lest you think that you are the only one struggling with titles, be assured that almost all writers do. For example, John Steinbeck's original title for *Of Mice and Men* was *Something That Happened.* Now there's a title to produce a yawn.

Oh, yes, my final title for my plant story: "I'm Too Young To Die." And in case you didn't notice, the title of this chapter is a take-off on Shakespeare's line "the play's the thing."

Chapter 8:

Fabricating Fabulous Fiction

While some nonfiction techniques are useful in fiction writing, there are some others that are needed. This chapter will give you the additional techniques you need to get started writing salable fiction.

Conflict

Conflict is the backbone of any story. Without conflict there is no plot to keep readers turning the pages. There are ten basic conflicts used in storytelling. One or more will be in every well-written story.

Basic Conflicts

1. **Man against man.** This, of course, includes woman against woman and woman against man. It is a conflict between people.

2. **Man against nature.** A man or woman may be alone or with others, but the basic conflict is against the elements, such as mountain climbing.

3. **Man against circumstances.** The protagonist must fight a combination of circumstances that may threaten his very life or at least his happiness.

4. **Man against society.** He may be trying to get society to change something it is doing or to start doing something it isn't, such as stop using nuclear reactions and start saving the environment.

5. **Man against himself.** This is an internal conflict, a should-I-or-shouldn't-I, what-am-I-to-do? kind of conflict.

6. **Man against the clock.** Whatever needs doing has a time limit or it will be too late. There's a ticking bomb to defuse or a child to rescue who is standing on the railroad tracks with a train barreling down on him.

7. **Man against changing times.** The protagonist wants things to stay the way they are. He may be right or wrong. Some change is good, some change isn't.

8. **Man against age.** This is a battle we all fight to a greater or lesser degree. To have conflict, the person has no desire to grow old gracefully.

9. **Man against God.** This is a battle that has been waged since the beginning of time. In mythology, man often fought against his gods.

10. **Man against the Unknown.** The protagonist does not know what to expect, but ventures forth bravely (or not so bravely).

Point of View

The point of view character is the narrator of the story. He (or she) may be a major or minor character, but the events are seen through his eyes and how he interprets them. Who the point of view character will be is a decision you, the writer, must make. The point of view you choose can drastically affect the story. The narrating character will set the tone. The same event can look quite different to different people.

Example:

A store is having a going out of business sale. To the owner it is the end of his dreams. To his wife it is a chance to do something she'd rather do than help run a business. To their children it is a loss of security. To the banker it's another loan to foreclose. To the customers it's a chance to get real bargains.

Point of View Limitations

A limit of the single character viewpoint narration is that he does not know what the other characters actually think. You must be careful not to have the viewpoint character reveal the actual thoughts of other characters. He will not know them. However, if it is important to reveal these other characters' thoughts, you can do so through dialogue with the characters saying what they think. In addition, the viewpoint character cannot see how she looks, for example, "her eyes sparkled."

You can also switch viewpoint characters for a time, but do so only when a clear division, such as a chapter break or line space denoting a time change occurs.

First Person Narration

A first person narration, of course, uses first person pronouns. "I was strolling down the sidewalk when I spotted trouble with a capital T." A problem beginning writers encounter when using first person narration is that all their narrators sound alike and usually like themselves. It is important that you know your characters so well that you know how they would talk. You then write your story like that.

Another limitation of first person narration is that the narrator must be present for all the main action. If he gets his information secondhand, it will bog down the story and take away from its believability.

Third Person Limited

The third person voice limited works basically the same way as first person except that it is written using such third person pronouns as he, she, or they, instead of first person ones. First person pronouns would still be used when writing dialogue.

Omniscient Point of View

If it is important to know what all the characters are thinking, then you will want to use the omniscient all-knowing point of view. You then can tell what each character thinks without your readers wondering how you know so much. With the omniscient viewpoint you can take the readers inside all the characters' minds. Readers then will have information other characters do not have.

Getting Started with Fiction

To get your creative juices flowing, write an opening paragraph with some kind of action and mystery. Mystery does not necessarily involve a crime. It can be something readers don't understand. It must hook the readers.

After you write your lead, try rewriting it from different viewpoints and see how that changes the focus of the story. As you change narrators, you may discover story possibilities you never dreamed existed.

Plot

Plot has been defined as what happens in a story. This definition is fine in describing the story after it is written. However, it doesn't help when you are *writing* a story. English novelist E. M. Forester has defined the difference between a plot and a story as follows: "We have defined a story as a narrative of events arranged in their time sequence. A plot is also a narrative of events, the emphasis falling on the causality. 'The King died and then the Queen died' is a story. 'The King died and then the Queen died of grief' is a plot."

Plot includes what the characters think, feel, say, and do. But to become a plot, what the characters do *must* affect future events. This is especially important in short story writing, where words are at a premium and you dare not waste them. Characters and dialogue should not wander aimlessly about. Each action or piece of dialogue should have some bearing, however small, on the outcome of the story. For example, if Lucy had not found the door to Narnia in the wardrobe, it would have been pointless for C. S. Lewis to tell about the children's game of hide-and-seek in *The Lion, the Witch, and the Wardrobe.*

List three or four pivotal events that could generate a story. It might be a wedding, a funeral, a car or train collision, or a criminal trial. Write an opening paragraph with one or more of the events playing a prominent role.

The middle of your story contains the main plot. It includes the conflicts and problems the characters face and how they work their way out of them. The middle should *show* the problems. As much as possible, action should be presented in chronological order. Use intriguing dialogue and vivid descriptions to make your story fascinating and move the plot along.

As you write the story, you must include conflict and characters who make readers care. If they are going to continue reading, they must want the conflict resolved *satisfactorily*. Satisfactorily does not necessarily mean the hero and heroine ride off into the sunset and live happily ever after. Satisfactorily does mean that the conflict is resolved in a way that is logical given the events in the story. The ending may be happy or tragic or a combination. No one would accuse Shakespeare of putting happy ever after endings on his tragedies, but they end satisfactorily.

In addition, you must care about your story idea. If you don't care about the characters and their conflicts, your readers won't either. As you think about your intended plot, ask yourself if it is going anywhere. Does the conflict even seem to want to be resolved? If not, there is no plot and therefore no story.

Where Do Plots Come From?

Happy people don't make good stories. Wait a minute, you say, in situation comedies on television, the characters are happy and there is a good story every week. Ah, yes, but there also is a conflict that *could* jeopardize their happiness, and therein lies the plot. Without conflict there is no story. Thus, even a situation comedy has conflict. Sometimes it is a struggle for control, dissatisfaction with the status quo, or tough decisions to be made. Conflict is the fabric of plotting.

We writers are often advised to write what we know best, which is good advice to a point. Sometimes we have to take what we know and concoct plots that have little basis in our own experiences. Science fiction writers have not had the experiences they write about. They start with a germ of reality and let their imaginations take it from there. When someone asked Mark Twain how much of his stories were based on fact, he replied that they were ten percent reality and ninety percent embroidery, and he wasn't writing science fiction.

Showing Not Telling

A major problem beginning fiction writers encounter is *telling* what happened rather than *showing* it. The germ of the story is there, but it is told and the readers are bored.

Instead of telling, you need to create scenes that allow the characters to show their emotions, act out their concerns and encounter, and overcome their problems. Ansen Dibell, in her book *Plot* defines *scene* as "one connected and sequential action, together with its embedded description and background material." She adds that it must be there for a reason and that it must be going somewhere. A scene's purpose is to move the plot along and to help explain the characters.

Know Your Destination

Although you may change direction and even the ending as you write, you need to have an idea of where you are going, the route you will take, and your final destination. If you don't, you can find yourself wandering, hopelessly lost, with no idea of where you are or where you're going.

As with nonfiction writing, you should be able to sum up your story idea in a sentence or two. If you can't, there is no focus. Think about some of the short stories or novels you have read and briefly state the basic plot. The guides to television viewing do that constantly. They state the basic plot very briefly. Reading them can give you ideas for solidifying your story summaries.

Characters

One purpose of fiction is to give insights into life, our human natures, and the way we behave that is not possible to get from real life. In real life, we often judge a person by what we see him do, and how she dresses. We make instant and sometimes wrong judgments. However, we usually do not investigate our decision.

In fiction, the writer can have the person do something that will generate a negative response from readers. You then take your readers behind the scenes and show them why the person behaved that way. For example, if you have a character who appears to think he is better than everyone else, your readers will develop an instant dislike for him. But, if you then show that he has had a really tough life and actually feels very insecure, you will have developed some sympathy for him. Your readers still may not be crazy about him, but they can empathize with his feelings of inferiority and will be more tolerant of his behavior.

Know Your Characters

Before you start writing, whether it is a short story or a novel, you must become thoroughly acquainted with your main character or characters. What do they look like? How do they talk? What kind of mannerisms do they have? What kind of family do they come from? You need to know them as well as you know yourself. Then, when you put conflicts into their lives, you instinctively will know how they are going to react. You will not have them do or say things that would be out of character.

Unless you are writing a melodrama, you do not want to create the flawless heroine or the completely despicable villain. Since there is good and bad, to greater or lesser degrees, in all of us, you need to include some flaws in the good guy and at least one or two likeable qualities in your bad guy. At their final confrontation, even Darth Vader exhibited fatherly love for his son Luke.

Also, if you put your characters in life and death situations and they need some extraordinary physical skill to get out of them, set the stage ahead of time. Show them practicing or somehow otherwise engaged in developing the skill that will save them. Your readers will not accept your heroine using karate to subdue a crazed rapist unless you have earlier shown that she is proficient in the martial arts.

Or you can have your character unable to do something and then use this lack of ability to create tension in the story. In *Jaws,* Peter Benchley lets readers know that Sheriff Brody cannot swim and doesn't even like the water. Thus, when he has to go out to face The Shark, more suspense exists than if he at least could swim.

When you get a story idea, don't just jot it down and think that's all you need to do. Examine it closely. Ask why it would happen. Then ask what could happen as a result. Keep going until you get away from the mundane story and come up with a new plot twist that will keep your readers turning the pages. You want to write a story they can't put down. I recently bought a novel that a friend advised me not to start reading after 8:00 p.m. because I would be up all night. It was that compelling. To write like that, you must create believable characters and make your readers care about what happens to them. You then must put them into seemingly impossible situations. However, if you put insurmountable problems in your protagonists' way and then get them out in an unbelievable manner, you will lose your readers.

Create Situations and Settings

When creating situations and settings for your characters, don't overlook what you consider ordinary. We think the place where we live is boring and uninteresting. We think we need to travel to exotic, or at least different, locales to find story settings. The truth is your readers may think your area is exciting because it is so different from where they live: The grass-is-greener syndrome. I know the first time I visited the Flint Hills of northeast Kansas, I mentioned their beauty to my cousin. She looked startled because she had been born and raised there and had never really noticed their beauty.

Keep your writer's eyes open. Observe. Observe. Observe. Sit on a park bench and watch people. Make up little vignettes about them. Stand in line at the grocery store or bank and observe your fellow customers. Are any doing something even slightly out of the ordinary? Could you exaggerate the action to make a plot? Jot the ideas down in your ever present notebook; don't wait until you get home or you will have lost the intensity of the moment.

When creating characters, writing about who you know can get you into deep trouble, and can cause real family problems if you recreate your eccentric aunt or impossible brother so they can recognize themselves. You may take characteristics and mannerisms from them, but disguise them. The aunt could become a man and you could give him one of her quirks and add others drawn from other people. Above all, don't tell someone you are basing a fictional character on him or her. That's a great way to alienate friends and family.

Naming Your Characters

What's in a name? That depends on you. The surname you give your characters can give readers a clue as to ethnic background. That name will bring with it all the stereotyped ideas readers have about that particular group.

Examples: Kasakowski, Johnson, O'Neill, Ortega

You should give characters names readers will remember. They should be different enough from each other so that readers can easily tell them apart. For example, don't have a protagonist named Joan and an antagonist named Jean. The names are too similar and will cause confusion. To help avoid confusion, start each character's name with a different letter.

The name also can tell readers something about the person. For example, a female character named *Ginger* should have a feisty disposition. Try to avoid the everyday common names. However, don't go to the other extreme and create names only you can pronounce.

In addition, to help keep your readers oriented, have your narrator call each character by one particular name all of the time. For example, if you have a character named Dr. Clayton R. Thomas and one time the narrator calls him "Dr. Thomas" and the next time "C. R." and a third time "Clayton," readers will become confused. They do not like to waste time trying to decide whom you're talking about.

Names also give your characters personality. Jot down names you hear and especially like. You never know when you can use them. As you read well-known authors, study the names they gave their characters. Try and decide how the names helped create characterization. Charles Dickens was a master of names. Can you imagine Ebenezer Scrooge being named Henry Johnson? Ebenezer Scrooge sounds mean (it's onomatopoeic).

Names can be used as symbols. Some, like Patience or Angel, are rather obvious and look affected to today's readers. However, names do need to sound the part. You would not name a macho character Perceval any more than you would call a very feminine heroine Roberta.

Look through the telephone directory for name ideas. Not only can you find potential character names, but the "Yellow Pages" can yield creative business names as well. While you may not want to use real names, you can get ideas that will help you create your own.

Dialogue

Well-written dialogue goes almost unnoticed by readers, while poorly written dialogue grabs their attention and can cause them to spit out the hook. Like everything else you write, dialogue must have a purpose. It is not there just to fill up space. It should be moving the story along by showing something about your characters, their relationship to each other, or conflict between them.

Practice writing dialogue. Create a conflict between two characters. Let the dialogue show the problem to the readers. Include at least two gestures or mannerisms that indicate the speaker's feelings toward the other character or the situation.

Create imaginary dialogue between you and someone else or between two other people. If you see two strangers involved in an animated discussion but cannot hear what is being said, make up dialogue. Keep the dialogue going as long as you can. You may be surprised at the number of unusual turns imaginary dialogues can take. You can create similar conditions in your living room by pressing the mute button on your television and then making up dialogue and a story to go with the action on the screen. Keep the dialogues you have created for future reference.

While good dialogue should sound natural, it cannot directly imitate life. *Really* listen to the next conversation you have. Would your readers be interested in hearing it verbatim? Probably not, unless it is more exciting than most of mine.

Also, you don't want to imitate real conversation too closely because most of us speak in sentence fragments, and even the most educated will sometimes drop the final *g* on *going* or other verb forms. We also repeat certain phrases like "you know," and readers don't want to read a lot of "you knows" in the dialogue. Readers want to see dialogue as we *should* speak.

They also do not want to wade through heavy dialect. Sometimes dialect is difficult to understand even when you hear it. Imagine how hard it is to read. Use just enough words to give the flavor of the dialect, then go back to standard English.

Example of difficult to understand dialect:

"Dere is somet'ing dere," he affirmed, when the rhythmed vagaries of his mind touched the secret chorts of Batard's being and brought forth the long lugubrious howl. "Ah pool eet out wid bot' my han's, so, an' so. Ha! Ha! Eet is fonee! Eet is ver' fonee! De priest chant, de womans pray, de mans swear, de leetle bird go *peep-peep*, Batard, heem go *yow-yow*—an' eet is all de oer' same t'ing. Ha! Ha!

[Jack London, "Batard"]

While dialogue can give readers needed information without the use of exposition, sometimes exposition is better. If the characters know each other quite well, you cannot have them stand around and tell each other facts they already know just to inform your readers. For example, you should not have a wife telling her husband that their son, Harold, who went away to college, then joined the Navy, became a fighter pilot, served in the Korean War, got married and has three children, two boys and a girl, is coming for a visit. That would be ridiculous. The only information the father might lack would be that Harold was coming for a visit. It would be better to give the rest as exposition— if it is important to the story.

Just as real people all have slightly different ways of expressing themselves, so should your characters. You can give them little quirks or speech mannerisms that are distinctly theirs. Personality differences should show through. Also, keep in mind that just as we speak differently in different situations such as work, home, church, ball game, so should your characters. Be sure the dialogue fits the situation.

In addition, while we sometimes ramble when we speak, you must condense what your characters have to say to the bare necessities. As Joe Friday says, "Just the facts, Ma'am." Also, as you revise, be sure your dialogue is free of cliches and other overworked expressions, unless you have picked one or two as speech mannerisms for a character.

Finally, don't have your characters continually call each other by name. We don't talk that way and neither should your characters. Reread your dialogue to see if you have done this.

Example:

"Hi, George, nice weather we're having."

"It's great, Zeke. I was able to get all my wheat harvested last week."

"That's wonderful, George. I'll finish mine tomorrow."

"That's good to hear, Zeke. Stop over sometime."

"I'll sure do that, George. Say hello to the Missus for me."

If only two characters are talking, quotation marks and paragraph changes should alert your readers to speaker changes. If necessary, you can add a "he said" occasionally to keep readers oriented. With three or more speakers you may need to add more "she says," but keep the names out of the dialogue itself.

As you check your dialogue, be sure:

1. It has a reason for being there. It is showing characterization or moving the plot along in some other way.

2. It does not have heavy dialect or other idiosyncrasies that will annoy readers.

3. Characters are not giving each other information they already know. If so, replace it with exposition.

4. Each character has some speech mannerisms all his own.

5. To cut out any rambling. There is no place for it in written speech.

6. The characters don't constantly refer to each other by name.

Flashbacks

A flashback interrupts the narration with a scene that recounts events or situations that occurred prior to the beginning of the story or before some event within the story itself. They are useful when you have started the story after something happened the readers need to know to understand the present action or why characters behave a certain way. Readers only want background information after you have aroused their curiosity. Resist the temptation to tell all you know. Make it as short as possible, then get back to the main action.

A principle value of the flashback is allowing the characters to tell the story rather than you, the writer, stepping in to tell what had happened. Flashbacks can slow the story down and often are awkward. Your story will benefit if the action flows along without your interference. However, unless a flashback is done well, it can harm your story rather than help it. So, before discussing how to use flashbacks, here are some ways to avoid them, if possible.

Avoiding the Flashback

First, try to start your story at an earlier point in time and tell it in a more chronological order. Or perhaps you can work the necessary information into the story naturally using a brief dialogue with characters discussing the details you want the readers to know.

Example:

"She really loved James," sighed Brenda.

"Yes, that's true." replied Sharon. "I remember the time..."

Now two of the characters are supplying the needed information. However, too much of this can become tedious and bog down the story. Use it sparingly.

Using the Flashback

Often flashbacks are unavoidable. If handled well, they can add to the story. But don't give away the ending before starting the flashback. For example, if you start your story with your character being sixty years old and then flashback to her youth and have her in life or death situations, the tension is gone as readers already know she survived.

Be sure the information you present is interesting enough that your readers will be willing to leave the present action. Readers will become aggravated if you take a flashback detour and it doesn't give them a feeling of involvement and make them want to keep reading.

It also is extremely important to choose the right place for the flashback. You do not want to put it in the middle of a scene with your protagonist in a life or death situation. Since readers are not sure he is going to make it out alive, they do not care how he came to be in such a precarious situation. They want him out of it. Readers will be extremely annoyed if you stop exciting action for a flashback. While a sponsor may be able to interrupt a television story at an exciting point in the action for a commercial—that's how they try to make sure you stay tuned—a writer cannot get away with interrupting exciting action for a flashback. Get the protagonist out of immediate danger, then while the problem may not be completely resolved but nothing is life-threatening, you can have him sit down and think about how he got into the mess in the first place. Or he could describe his experience to someone and tell how he'd managed to get into so much trouble.

Getting Into the Flashback

One method you can use to get into a flashback is with sensory impressions. All of us have experienced momentary trips into the past triggered by a long-forgotten sight, sound, or smell. A picture in a photo album, the fragrance of a certain perfume, the aroma of steaks on the grill, or the sound of a carousel may remind us of special events in our lives. You can use the same technique with your characters to have them remember what it is you want to tell your readers.

Since most fiction is written in the past tense, it is necessary to use the past perfect *had* to establish the fact that you are moving further back in time.

Example:

> Jean gazed out the window at the softly falling rain. It had
> been a day much like this when Sam had left for the Army. He had
> looked so handsome in his uniform.

Now that you have established that the action is in the past, you can go back to using past tense until you are ready to bring the action back to the present. Then use enough *hads* to remind readers they have been in the past and now are moving back to the present.

Also, be sure to keep readers oriented as to time and place. Words like *yesterday* and *when he was twelve* remind readers they are in the past. Used at the beginning of a flashback, they help readers know immediately how far back you are taking them. An extra space between paragraphs also can alert readers you are moving them ahead or back in time. When adding this extra line in your manuscript, place three asterisks in the middle of the line so the editor will know you have intentionally included the extra line.

Example: * * *

While flashbacks usually are not long, occasionally almost an entire story or novel is a flashback. One such successful novel is John Knowles' *A Separate Peace.* He is careful not to give away important information before the flashback. While Knowles foreshadows *someone's* death just before the flashback begins he does not say who it will be. He states: "Nothing endures, not a tree, not love, not even a death by violence." However, if before going into the flashback Knowles had had narrator Gene think about how the tree reminded him of Finney's death, the shock of his death near the end would be gone. Knowles would have robbed readers of much of their interest in the plot because they already would know that no matter what else happened, Finney would die an untimely, violent death.

In *A Separate Peace,* as Knowles moved his readers into the flashback, he set the stage by comparing how the tree, which played a significant part in the plot, looked first to Gene as a grown man and then to him as a frightened sixteen-year-old.

Before the flashback:

> …Unbelievable that there were other trees which looked like it here. It had loomed in my memory as a huge lone spike dominating the riverbank, forbidding as an artillery piece, high as the beanstalk. Yet here was a scattered grove of trees, none of them of any particular grandeur.

> …This was the tree, and it seemed to me standing there to resemble those men, the giants of your childhood, whom you encounter years later and find that they are not merely smaller in relation to your growth, but that they are absolutely smaller, shrunken by age. In this double demotion the old giants have become pigmies while you were looking the other way.

Starting the flashback:

> The tree was tremendous, an irate, steely black steeple beside the river.

Make moving in and out of flashbacks as painless as possible. You do not want readers to feel they are being yanked from one time and place to another and back again. Nor do you want them to have to stop to figure out if they are in a flashback or present action.

Several years ago, I read a novel that continually switched between the present and past and back again. I became completely disoriented because most of the time I wasn't sure whether the action was in the present or the past and thus wasn't sure what was happening. If it had not been assigned reading for a class, I am sure I would not have read past the first chapter.

Flashback Test

As you write flashbacks, examine them to be sure they pass the following five-point test. If so, they should be painless and your readers will not feel they are being yanked around.

1. Did you include the flashback only after trying all possible ways to avoid it?

2. Did you put the flashback in a place that is not going to interrupt some action the readers are very interested in?

3. Did you eliminate the past perfect had except at the beginning and end?

4. Did you put in only the *really* necessary information and overcome the temptation to tell readers more than they need or want to know?

5. Did you put the basic information in plain sight so the readers don't have to search for it?

If you cannot answer yes to all five questions, you need to do some more revising.

Foreshadowing

Foreshadowing is another useful fiction writing technique. It gives clues that something will happen later and helps make those events more believable. In other words, you plant information in your story.

Foreshadowing can be divided into two parts. First, the promise; then, the delivery on the promise. Like flashbacks, foreshadowing should be painless and not interrupt the flow of the story. Also, you do not want to speak directly to your readers, e.g., "Little did Abigail know how moving to Atlanta was going to change her life." Or, "If only Joshua had known ..." These are too obvious. Well-done foreshadowings plant hints subtly.

Foreshadowings tell readers to pay close attention. *Something* is going to happen. It also keeps you, the writer, on track because you must produce on any promises you have planted in the story. Each time you plant a foreshadowing, you are forced to include plot complications, reversals, and conflicts to bring it to a satisfactory conclusion. It is a good idea when planting foreshadowings to write yourself a note so you will fulfill your promise before the end of the story. You may keep these notes in a notebook or arrange the plot chapter by chapter on poster board. The latter lets you see at a glance what has been fulfilled and what remains to be done.

The foreshadowing can involve major or minor incidents and can be fulfilled soon or left unfulfilled until much later in the story. For example, in chapter 4 of *Silas Marner,* George Eliot foreshadows a major incident, Dunstan's death in the stone pit. However, his body is not discovered and the foreshadowing fulfilled until chapter 18.

Death foreshadowed in chapter 4:

> Dunstan Cass, setting off in the raw morning... passed by the piece of unenclosed ground called the stone pit, where stood the cottage... The spot looked very dreary at this season, with the moist trodden clay about it, and the red, muddy water high up in the deserted quarry.

> ... Dunstan's own recent difficulty in making his way suggested to him that the weaver had perhaps gone outside his cottage to fetch in fuel,... and had slipped into the stone pit.

> ... The rain and darkness had got thicker, and he [Dunstan] was glad of it; though it was awkward walking... But when he had gone a yard or two, he might take his time. So he stepped forward into the darkness.

Fulfilled, chapter 18:

> ... "It's Dunstan—my brother Dunstan, that we lost sight of sixteen years ago. We've found him—found his body—his skeleton."
>
> "The stone pit has gone dry suddenly—from the draining, I suppose; and there he lies—has lain for sixteen years, wedged between two great stones..."

On the other hand, Margaret Landon foreshadows a rather minor incident in chapter 13 of *Anna and the King of Siam* and fulfills it a few pages later. First hint of trouble:

> The only omission was material suitable for undergarments. When Anna remonstrated with the chamberlain on her neglect, she simply replied that there was not time to make any.

If that had been the only mention of the lack of undergarments her readers would not necessarily have expected trouble.

Two pages later:

> Anna knew a brief pang of regret that there had been no time for undergarments, although a critical examination reassured her that the heavy brocades were so thick that no one could possibly have guessed the omission.

Since Landon has mentioned the lack of undergarments twice, a problem appears to be coming.

Fulfilled three pages later:

> And with one accord they started up from their seats, threw their skirts over their heads to protect them, and fled from the temple.

Had nothing happened, the reader would have wondered why so much concern over the lack of undergarments and would have felt Landon had used a false foreshadowing.

False Foreshadowing

In *false foreshadowing* a writer hints at something to come and then does not deliver on the promise. Sometimes this is used in mystery stories to throw readers off the criminal's trail. However, there is unwarranted false foreshadowing in the Batman movie when The Joker (Jack Nicholson) tells Vicki Vale (Kim Basinger) his life's goal: "I want my picture on the dollar bill." The audience has been told Joker's ambition, so later when he announces he will pass out millions of dollars on a specified night, we expect him to use bills with his picture on them. Instead he uses real money and no explanation is given as to why he hadn't had money printed with his picture on it and then passed it out. This is false foreshadowing. An expectation is raised and then is not met.

Keep Track of Details

As you write, you need to keep track of details you have included. Readers love to play detective as they read. They look for places you have slipped up so they can tell you about it. For example, if you have a character who is a blonde on page six, she should still be a blonde on page seventy-two, unless you have had her change her hair color and told the readers she did it.

Now, it's time for you to dust off that story idea and use what you have learned. Do as the March Hare and the Mad Hatter told Alice in *Alice in Wonderland,* "Begin at the beginning, go on 'til you come to the end. Then stop." Happy story-telling.

Chapter 9:

Transitions = Strong Word Bridges

If you don't want to get your feet wet when crossing a stream, you look for a bridge and walk across on it. If there is no bridge and the stream is narrow enough, you might decide to construct one yourself.

Just as a bridge lets you cross a body of water without getting wet, so word bridges—better known as transitions—allow your readers to cross from one idea to another without slipping and falling in between ideas.

Transitions are important tools in the writer's toolbox. They help make writing smooth so the reader doesn't fall into a stream of disconnected thoughts or bump along a rocky road of paragraphs, because a word bridge isn't there to help them make a smooth crossing.

Transitions are used to tie all parts of writing together. For example, they may be used to connect two parts of a sentence so readers will clearly understand its meaning. In some cases, if there is no transitional word or phrase, readers may be confused. However, worse than no transition is a wrong transition because it can add to the confusion.

Let's look at the following sentence, first without a transition, then with a wrong transition, and finally with a proper transition.

"Most students did poorly on the test, Laura scored ninety percent."

Without a transition the meaning is unclear. Is ninety percent considered a poor performance?

Now let's add a wrong transition.

"Most students did poorly on the test; *for example,* Laura scored ninety percent."

This is even more confusing. Most people would agree that ninety percent is not a bad score, yet the sentence indicates that it isn't good.

Let's try again.

"*Although* most students did poorly on the test, Laura scored ninety percent."

Now the meaning is clear. Laura's score is one of the few exceptions. The sentence also could be written:

"Most students did poorly on the test; *however,* Laura scored ninety percent."

As Connectors Within

In addition, transitions can connect ideas within a paragraph so that the paragraph flows smoothly. We see this in the following example:

> "There are many roads that you can take to Washington, D.C. For example, if you are on a sightseeing trip, you might take...However, if you are in a hurry, you will want to take..."

Notice how each sentence blends into the next. Reread the sentences without the italicized transitions and see how they bump along from thought to thought.

The following paragraph suffers from a lack of smooth transitions:

> The view from the veranda was breathtaking. There was an immaculately kept garden with many varieties of exotic tropical plants. Tiny birds darted from flower to flower. The sun cast its golden rays over the Pacific Ocean. A sailboat added to the beauty of the scene. Children laughed and played on the beach. I wished the scene could last forever. Darkness soon settled on the scene as though someone had dropped a heavy blanket over the only light in the room.

Because of the lack of transitions, the reader cannot be sure where the different parts of the scene are located. Notice how it is improved with the addition of transitions in the following rewrite:

> The view from the veranda was breathtaking. *Just below* was an immaculately kept garden with many varieties of exotic tropical plants. *Here and there* tiny birds darted from flower to flower. *Straight ahead past the garden wall,* the sun cast its golden

> rays over the Pacific Ocean. *To my left near the horizon* a sailboat
> added to the beauty of the scene, *while to my right* children laughed
> and played on the beach. I wished the scene could last forever.
> *However,* darkness soon settled on the scene as though someone
> had dropped a heavy blanket over the only light in the room.

Now the paragraph flows smoothly and the scene is in focus. The reader knows the spatial location of each item being described.

Pronouns also can be used to tie sentences or paragraphs together by referring to the person, place, thing, or idea in the previous sentence. *He, she, it, they, this, that, these, those,* and *them* are some pronouns frequently used this way. Using pronouns as adjectives also can serve this purpose: *this* theory, *these* opinions, *those* tactics.

In the following paragraph each italicized pronoun links the sentence to the one preceding it.

As Connectors Without

> He understood fully that he might actually be going to die;
> his arms, maintaining his balance on the ledge, were trembling
> steadily now. And it occurred to him then with all the force of a
> revelation that, if he fell, all he was ever going to have out of life
> he would then, abruptly, have had.
>
> ["Contents of the Dead Man's Pockets", Jack Finney]

Just as transitions are important within the body of a paragraph, they are necessary when moving from one paragraph to another. The reader needs to know immediately how each paragraph is related to the one preceding it.

Several methods are available for you to take your readers between paragraphs without getting their feet wet. You can:

1. Repeat the main idea from the preceding paragraph as the opening sentence of the next one.

2. Repeat a key word from the preceding paragraph in the new paragraph.

3. Ask your readers a question.

4. Build on connecting words. However, be sure to read your material aloud to see if you have overused this method. Also, be aware of connecting words that stand out because you have used them too often. In addition, check for ones that don't sound natural. Your readers should not be consciously aware that they are being taken from one idea to the next.

5. Use a phrase that connects the two ideas.

6. Simply tell your readers you are moving from one subject to another. If you are contrasting information, you might use "despite that," or "on the other hand."

7. Set up solid divisions by breaking the article down into sections with subtitles, numbers, or bullets. Your readers then will know you are changing the subject.

8. Finally, if you just can't seem to find a transition that will fit, it could be that the paragraph or section is not in its logical order. Try moving it somewhere else in the article or story. If that doesn't work, maybe it isn't closely enough related to the main idea and needs to be taken out. Don't completely discard it as you may be able to incorporate it into a sidebar or another piece of writing.

Now let's examine some ways to get between paragraphs. For instance, let's say an article is being written on the advantages and disadvantages of certain types of hobbies. As the paragraph describing one hobby is finished, the writer moves on to the next hobby. The following is an example of what the last line in the paragraph might be:

"Collecting this kind of stamp can be quite expensive."

Possibly, the next paragraph is about model airplane building.

"Model airplane building doesn't require much money."

No continuity exists here. The move has been made from stamp collecting to model airplane building with no transitional bridge. The writer needs to build a bridge to get readers from stamps to model airplanes, otherwise the readers will get their feet wet.

There are many ways to build that bridge. The new paragraph might start:

"Model airplane building, *on the other hand,* can be quite inexpensive." Or: *"Unlike stamp collecting,* model airplane building is quite inexpensive." Or: *"However, if you don't want to invest a lot of money,* model airplane building may be for you."

Connectors in Fiction

So far the transition methods, while usable in fiction, are basically for nonfiction. Now, let's look at some ways to move action ahead in fiction without losing readers in the creek or boring them with unnecessary detail.

Transitions in fiction need to be even more subtle than those in nonfiction. Readers should not be aware they are being moved from place to place or from time to time. The movement needs to be done in as few words as possible, although it must be clear and easy.

Chronological Method

One way to move time ahead is the chronological method. You tell the readers you have moved ahead, minutes, hours, or days.

Example:

> Joe grabbed his jacket and cap, kissed his wife, and dashed out the door. As he turned the key in the ignition, he shouted, "So long, hon. Have a good day!"
>
> Fifteen minutes later he tossed his jacket into his locker and headed for his workbench.

The "fifteen minutes later" saves us his trip.

Echo Method

Another method is the echo effect. While it is a little more difficult to master then the chronological, it is quite useful. In the echo effect a word in one scene echoes a word from the preceding scene, making a bridge for the readers to cross.

Example:

> Amanda slammed her desk drawer shut. She would not retype that letter for the fifth time, not if old Robertson pleaded on bended knee. It was lunch time, and if Robertson didn't appreciate her abilities, *Jim would.*
>
> Jim did. As they devoured ham sandwiches, Amanda talked...

Amanda has moved from the office to the restaurant. *Jim did* echoes *Jim would* and saves us her travel to the restaurant.

The echo effect can be used frequently without getting stale. Too many uses of "fifteen minutes later" can become tiresome. The echo also can be used to span longer periods of time. This long-range echo is similar to the simple echo. However, it takes a little more thought and work.

Example:

> Marcia enjoyed the long, lazy days of summer. The hot sun added to her already golden tan as she lounged by the shimmering blue waters of the lake. It was relaxing to watch the white puffs of clouds drift through the clear blue sky. She loved watching the birds and trying to spot their homes hidden in the green foliage of the trees. She was content.
>
> * * *
>
> Now that was all changed. The sun occasionally peeked out through an overcast gray sky. The blue of the lake had lost its luster and the birds had flown south for the winter, leaving the bare branches of the trees reaching toward the forbidding sky almost as if they were asking to have their green protection back. Even Marcia's beautiful tan was starting to fade. The approach of winter always made Marcia restless. She sometimes thought of it as her season of discontent.

Here, since it is a longer time span, it takes more than just the few words of the simple echo. However, at the end of each paragraph the echo is still there. In addition, the extra space between the paragraphs indicates the passage of time.

While it can be used to move ahead in time as in the example above, an echo also can move the action from one place to another. Let's say you moved a character ahead in time and from the city to the country. You could contrast the sights, sounds, and smells found in each as a transitional bridge.

Example:

> In five days—if everything went well—Frederick would be in the country. He shrank from the heat as the blistering sun bounced off the pavement, from the enraged screams, from the noise and the pollution, and from the taste of dust. It would be different in the country... *he hoped.*

* * *

> In the country the sun was just as hot, but it warmed rather than blistered. As Frederick jabbed his bare toes into the grass, he listened to the pigs grunting and the chickens cackling and to the constant drone of the tractor as his grandfather plowed up a field. He spotted a ripe cherry tomato, picked it, and popped it into his mouth. As some of the juice dribbled down his chin, *he grinned.*

Notice the pattern of the echoes: the feel of the sun, the noises, and the tastes. The pattern carries the reader five days forward in time. The recurring echoes prevent a time gap and the confusion it can cause. Again, an extra space is added denoting the passage of time.

Checking The Big Picture

Once you have the ideas within your sentences, between your sentences, and between your paragraphs tied together, you need to determine whether the main parts of your article or story are tied together. Transitions also can do this.

For example, if you are contrasting the United States and Soviet governments, you might discuss the Soviet's for several paragraphs. Then you will want to start contrasting our form of government. To make the change smoothly, the section on the Soviet government might end with the sentence: *"In conclusion, the Soviet government allows its citizens very limited freedom of speech."* Then to tie them together, the section on the United States government could begin:

"Unlike the Soviets, free speech in America is guaranteed by our Constitution."

The following examples are the way some writers have used paragraphs to get from one section to another:

> So much, then, by way of proof that the method of establishing laws in science is exactly the same as that pursued in common life. Let us now turn to another matter (though really it is but another phase of the same question), and that is, the method by which, from the relations of certain phenomena, we prove that some stand in the position of causes toward the others.
>
> [from "The Method of Scientific Investigation" by Thomas Henry Huxley.]

> The entries in an unabridged dictionary such as the *Webster's Third New International Dictionary,* however, differ in some respects from the entries in a college dictionary. Let us consider these differences.
>
> [English Grammar and Composition, Harcourt Brace Jovanovich, Franklin Edition c. 1982, p. 369-370.]

> Whereas at the beginning of *Pride and Prejudice* the reader sees Elizabeth as confident, even headstrong, in her opinions, later in the novel her self-assurance begins to falter. Take, for example, her meeting with Darcy at Rosings.
>
> [English Grammar, p. 370]

So, transitions are important to every phase of writing. As a reminder, here are some of the points covered.

1. Be careful to avoid vague or confusing transitions. They can be worse than no transition at all.

2. Read each sentence aloud for clarity and smoothness; then add appropriate transitions where necessary.

3. Tie each sentence within a paragraph together so that the relationship between the sentences is clearly shown.

4. When moving from paragraph to paragraph, be sure to keep the continuity of the article or story flowing smoothly by showing a relationship between the paragraphs.

5. Tie major divisions together so readers won't wonder how the sections are related to each other.

6. Keep in mind that a good transition is a subtle transition. Don't hit your readers over the head with the move. For example, don't use obvious movers like: "Meanwhile back at the ranch..."

Following these six basic steps to good transition use will improve your basic skills. And readers will have bridges to cross and be able to keep their feet dry.

A Selection of Transitional Words

Here are some transition words put into categories for ease of location. In some cases a transition can fit in more than one category.

Spatial Order:
above, across, adjacent, alongside, around, behind, below, beneath, beside, between, beyond, by, in front of, in the middle, opposite, throughout, under, upon, within

Order of Importance:
first, in the first place, a second factor, equally important, furthermore, of major concern, of minor concern, best of all, finally, least important, most important, just as important, above all, but more important

Comparison/Contrast:
equally, similarly, the same, in the same way, just as, likewise, in like manner, however, on the other hand, despite, otherwise, but, yet, conversely, on the contrary, unlike, nevertheless, contrary to, after all, although true, and yet, at the same time, in contrast, in spite of, notwithstanding, still

Cause and Effect:
affect, as a result, because, causes, consequently, then, effect, for, produces, results, therefore, why, so thus, accordingly, hence, in short, otherwise, truly

To show a time, place, or chronological order:
first, meanwhile, next, second, later, presently, finally, eventually, opposite to, sooner or later, adjacent to, in the beginning, then, prior, here, before, during, nearby, following, at length, at this point, afterward, at the end, soon, now, moments later, in the meantime, at the moment, formerly, at last, after a short time, as long as, as soon as, at that time, at the same time, earlier, of late, immediately, lately, shortly, since, temporarily, thereafter, thereupon, until, when, while

To add an idea to one already stated:
moreover, furthermore, besides, equally important, and, and then, in the same fashion, further, likewise, too, nor, again, in addition, also, finally, first, second, third, et cetera, last

To illustrate some idea or to sum up what has been said:
for example, in any event, in brief, in other words, as I have said, in short, to sum up, for instance, in any case, on the whole, in fact, as a result, in particular, namely, also, incidentally, indeed, specifically, that is, to illustrate

Concede a point:
granted that, no doubt, to be sure, after all, although this may be true, at the same time, even though, I admit, naturally, of course

Paraphrase or summary:
in other words, to conclude, to sum up, in conclusion, in brief, in short, on the whole, to summarize

Logical conclusion:
accordingly, consequently, as a result, hence

Using transitions effectively is the result of writing, editing, and rewriting. No part of writing comes easily. Professionalism is the result of hard work and many hours of study.

Transition Exercises

Now it's your turn to add the transitions.

The following sentences need at least one transition within or between them.

1. My father will not let me go out on school nights. I cannot go to the basketball game this Thursday.

2. Sally invited some friends over for a Christmas party. She invited some of her neighbors.

3. The tornado destroyed the bleachers at the football field. The championship game had to be postponed.

4. Jane planned to put $50 in her savings account. She decided to buy some new shoes.

5. The temperature reached 90 degrees; the pool was closed because of water pollution.

The following paragraphs need transitions to make their meaning clear.

1. Making chocolate chip cookies is easy. Get out your ingredients. Preheat the oven. Mix ingredients in the order given in the recipe. Bake the cookies to a golden brown. You and your family will enjoy the delicious results.

2. Sometime ago I visited a restored carousel in Abilene, Kansas. I was alone in the building, the music was playing. I stood there

transfixed thinking of all the laughing children who had ridden it in bygone days.

3. It was a typical Monday morning. The children did not want to get out of bed to go to school. The toast burned and the oatmeal boiled over. I went out to start the car and found I had a flat tire!

Between Paragraphs

You must move readers smoothly from one paragraph to another. See if you can move them smoothly between the following pairs of sentences. The first is the last sentence of one paragraph, and the second is the first sentence of the next.

1. Clean hands and fingernails, then, are essential to good grooming.

   People should pay attention to the appearance of their clothes.

2. People who can sew can also design their own clothes.

   They can make decorations for the home.

3. As these figures show, students can earn a great deal of spending money by delivering newspapers.

   They can make several dollars a week by baby-sitting.

Suggested Answers

Here are some ways that the previous exercises could be done. Remember, there can be several right ways to use transitions. The most important thing is not to use wrong ones.

Within and Between Sentences

1. My father will not let me go out on school nights. *Therefore,* I cannot go to the basketball game this Thursday.
2. Sally invited some friends over for a Christmas party; she invited some of her neighbors *as well.*
3. *Because* the tornado destroyed the bleachers at the football field, the championship game had to be postponed.
4. Jane planned to put $50 in her savings account. *However* she decided to buy some new shoes instead.
5. *Despite the fact that* the temperature reached 90 degrees, the pool was closed because of water pollution.

Transitions within Paragraphs

1. Making chocolate chip cookies is easy. *First,* get out your ingredients. *Then preheat the oven. Next,* mix ingredients in the order given in the recipe. *When thoroughly mixed,* drop by teaspoonfuls on a cookie sheet *and* bake the cookies to a golden brown. *Finally,* you and your family will enjoy the delicious results.
2. Sometime ago, I visited a restored carousel in Abilene, Kansas. *Although* I was alone in the building, the music was playing. *For several minutes* I stood there transfixed, thinking of all the laughing children who had ridden it in bygone days.
3. It was a typical Monday morning. *First* the children did not want to get out of bed to go to school. *While I was trying to get them up,* the toast burned and the oatmeal boiled over. *To top it all off,* when I went out to start the car, I found I had a flat tire!

Between Paragraphs

1. Well-groomed people also pay attention to the appearance of their clothes.
2. Besides being some of the best dressed people in the neighborhood, they can fill their homes with their own beautiful creations.
3. Perhaps you would rather earn money working with children. You could let parents of young children know you're available to baby-sit.

Chapter 10:

Polishing Your Prose

You have just finished your first draft. Congratulations. Now it's time to reach for your trusty market guide and see which lucky editor will get first chance to reject it. "Wait a minute!" you say. "Isn't that rather cynical? After all, I've done my research and writing and now I'm finished." WRONG. Your work has just begun. Most writing is rewriting. However, if you did a thorough job of prewriting and writing, the rewriting stage will be much less painful.

There is a common misconception that well-known writers do not rewrite. That is not true. Some rewrite as many as fourteen or fifteen times until it is just the way they want it. Lafcadio Hearn once revised a paragraph seventeen times, and Tolstoy kept rewriting until he caught himself replacing the vivid word with the dull.

George Bernard Shaw often sent the early drafts of his plays to his friend Ellen Terry, the actress, for criticism. Once she said she feared to suggest changes on his manuscript. He wrote back: "Oh, bother the manuscript, mark them as much as you like: what else are they for? Mark everything that strikes you. I may consider a thing forty-nine times; but if you consider it, it will be considered fifty times; and a line fifty times considered is two percent better than a line forty-nine times considered. And it is the final two percent that makes the difference between excellence and mediocrity."

I can hear you now: "But I just can't stand to revise this one more time; the more I read it the worse it sounds." As writers, we must often bore ourselves so we don't bore our readers. Our readers expect and deserve the very best we can give them—the excellence, not the mediocrity. Leonard Goss, editor at Zondervan Publishing states: "The success of any writer is in direct ratio to the number of times the writer goes back to write. Good writers are seldom satisfied with their first efforts."

Put Some Distance

Before you start revising, put some distance between you and your writing. Set it aside for a few days. Work on another writing project, or do something completely unrelated to writing. Then you will have a fresh perspective and you will be able to see flaws you missed the first time through.

None of our words are etched in granite. Don't cling to a pet word or phrase that doesn't seem to fit just because you like it. Save it, however, because it may work some other time and place. Examine your work as though your worst enemy wrote it and you really want to find things wrong with it.

Look at your writing through the eyes of a busy editor. He has a desk piled high with unsolicited manuscripts. What is it about your article or story that will make him stop and read it? You must play the devil's advocate for everything you write. Challenge the complete piece, the paragraphs, the sentences, and finally the individual words. Look at each part with a critical eye. Your story can be improved.

The Big Picture

To begin the revision process, look at the overall picture, the completed piece. Then, check it paragraph by paragraph, then, sentence by sentence, and, finally, word by word. After that, the manuscript is ready for a final proofreading for anything you may have missed along the way.

Some questions to ask yourself as you look at the big picture are:

1. What did you say? If you cannot sum up your main idea in a sentence or two, you have not focused your writing tightly enough. Your theme will not be clear to your readers.

2. Does it make sense? Have you said everything in an understandable way? Is everything presented in a logical sequence? Or will your readers put your article or story down wondering what it is all about?

3. If it is persuasive writing, did you use valid arguments, or will the other side be able to blow holes in them with no trouble at all?

4. Is it written as clearly as possible? Here is where another person's input is helpful. What may seem clear to you, since you know what you're talking about, may not be clear to someone else.

5. Does it move smoothly from beginning to end? Are there transitions to move readers effortlessly from one thought to the next?

6. Do your ideas and details support your primary purpose: to explain, describe, persuade, or tell a story?

7. Will your intended audience find it interesting?

8. Does it contain enough background information and explanation of terms to make it clear to your readers?

9. Conversely, have you included information your readers already know?

10. Have you grouped similar ideas or information together so your readers can find them easily?

11. Have you presented the ideas in a sequence that will make the main idea clear?

As you go over the big picture using this checklist, you may find problems. Here are some common problems and suggestions for correcting them:

Nonfiction

1. Some of the words you used do not fit the audience, tone, and purpose. Take them out and replace them with appropriate ones.

2. The tone changes within the piece. Constantly remind yourself of your intended audience, purpose, and tone.

3. The tone is not suitable for your intended audience. Cut words or ideas that make it improper and replace them with ones that fit your audience's knowledge, interests, age, and biases.

4. Some ideas and details do not help explain, describe, persuade, or tell the story. Cut out any information that does not relate to your purpose for writing. You may need to add explanations, supporting arguments such as statistics, a quote, or an anecdote, and descriptive or narrative details.

5. What you have written does not grab and keep the readers' attention. You need to add interesting anecdotes, examples, dialogue, or more narrative detail. Remember, show, don't tell.

6. Unfamiliar terms or jargon have not been explained to a general audience. Replace them with more familiar words whenever possible. Add an explanation of those terms you feel are necessary to leave in.

7. You have not included enough information so your intended audience can understand the topic. You will need to add details, facts, examples, explanations, or anecdotes to support what you have written. Conversely, don't give your readers information they already know.

8. Some information either does not support the topic or really has nothing to do with it. Irrelevant information will confuse and distract your readers, because they will be trying to figure out what the information has to do with your main idea. It may be part of a sentence, an entire sentence, or a paragraph. Cut out that information.

9. The information is not in a logical order. Move the information around until it is. If it is chronological, the events need to be presented so that they are in the order they happened. If it is a step-

by-step process, the steps need to be in the order performed. If you have some information that just doesn't seem to belong anywhere, then it probably doesn't belong at all. Take it out.

Fiction

10. The setting does not seem right for the characters and the conflict. Review your main characters and the conflicts you have brought into their lives. Then cut descriptions that are unrelated to one or the other and replace them with more appropriate descriptive details.

11. The action is not presented in an organized fashion. For example, you may find you have moved in and out of flashbacks too often. Rearrange events to eliminate confusion.

12. No feeling of suspense exists. Without some kind of conflict, you have no plot. Add some. Look for places in your story, especially as the action *rises,* where you can add details that contribute to the suspense. The detail may be another road block thrown in the path of your main character. Or, it can be another character or problem he will have to face before resolving the main conflict.

13. You find the point of view is inconsistent. Unless you are using the omniscient point of view, cut places where you find the narrator knows too much and replace those scenes with ones that are consistent with the intended point of view.

14. You find your characters are not fully developed. If they are flat, add details that will make them more rounded and suitable to the way you want to portray them. Then they will become more motivated and believable. Remember, no one believes the completely perfect hero or completely evil villain. Use dialogue and actions to reveal character traits.

15. Your dialogue does not sound natural. Cut any that sounds unnatural and replace inappropriate language with language suited to the characters and situations. For example, you would not have someone with a third grade education talk like a college English professor, using very proper grammar, nor would the professor speak like an uneducated person, saying things like, "I ain't going" or "He don't know."

Paragraph by Paragraph

Now that the big picture is under control, it is time to check each paragraph. As you do this, ask yourself:

1. Does each paragraph focus on a single person, place, object, or event? Does it state or imply a single main idea? Remember, each paragraph should have only one main idea. If you find more than one idea in a paragraph, you need to break the paragraph apart. On the other hand, you may find two closely related short paragraphs you can combine into one.

2. Is the most important information at the beginning and end of the paragraph? Remember, readers tend to scan as they read.

3. Have you included enough concrete and sensory details to enable your readers to experience the topic? The more senses involved, the more vivid the readers' impression will be.

4. Is each sentence related to the one just before and after it? Is each directly related to the main idea?

5. Are the ideas arranged in a logical order? If not, rearrange them. Make your ideas flow smoothly from one sentence to the next.

6. Use direct references and transitions to tie sentences together.

Sentence by Sentence

Now it's time to examine each sentence.

1. Are sentences varied in length and structure to avoid monotony?

2. Does each sentence contribute to the overall tone of the piece?

3. Does each sentence move the idea of the paragraph forward?

4. Is each sentence clearly written with just enough clauses to qualify and develop the subject?

5. Avoid starting a sentence with the same word that ended the preceding one. For example: They were searching for John. John was hiding in the ditch.

6. As you check your sentences search for and eliminate redundancy, deadwood, and wordiness.

Redundancy

Redundancy is the unnecessary repetition of an idea. Redundant words repeat the meaning of other words in the sentence. Adjectives that repeat the meaning of nouns, and adverbs that repeat the meaning of verbs should be eliminated.

Examples:

Redundant: He has studied past history extensively.

Concise: He has studied history extensively.

Redundant: They screamed loudly at the sight of the fake mouse.

Concise: They screamed at the sight of the fake mouse.

Redundant prepositional phrases can clutter sentences with ideas that have already been expressed.

Examples:

Redundant: Pat's face turned red in color, and he ran from the room.

Concise: Pat's face turned red, and he ran from the room.

Redundant: She had an idea in her mind that would solve the problem.

Concise: She had an idea that would solve the problem.

Redundant clauses can make sentences illogical or even pointless. They offer explanations that are not explanations— but repetitions of ideas in main clauses.

Examples:

Redundant: The television did not work because it was broken.

Concise: The television did not work.

Deadwood

Deadwood consists of unnecessary words that take up space without adding meaning. It includes hedging words, consisting of unnecessary qualifying expressions, and empty words that add nothing to your ideas.

Hedging words: it seems that, somewhat, it is my opinion that, I think that

Empty words: it is a fact that, it is also true that, despite the fact that, the thing is

Examples:

With deadwood: What I want for my birthday, I think, is a typewriter for the reason that I tend to type faster than I write.

Concise: For my birthday, I want a typewriter because I type faster than I write.

Wordiness

A wordy clause or phrase uses more words than necessary. Reduce a wordy clause or phrase to a shorter structure or to a single word. You want to use the simplest grammatical construction you can without losing the intended meaning. When possible, change a wordy clause to a concise phrase and a wordy phrase to a just right word.

Examples:

Wordy clause: The young man who was wrestling with the grocery cart looked confused.

Concise: The young man *wrestling with the grocery cart* looked confused.

Wordy phrase: Detectives discovered that the name of the suspect was Smith.

Concise: Detectives discovered that the *suspect's* name was Smith.

Word by Word

1. Have you used specific rather than general language? Are the figures of speech you used appropriate and effective? Have you replaced weak general words with strong specific ones? Are your descriptive words vivid?

2. Have you used figurative language where appropriate?

3. Do your words bore you? They will bore your readers too. Exchange them for vivid ones.

4. Look for excessive use of *be* verbs. See the grammar chapter for a discussion of *be* verbs. They cause an overuse of nouns and

adjectives and also lack force and liveliness. Eliminate as many as possible. Their use can add words like *it* and *there* to your writing.

5. For emphasis, have you used parallel construction where appropriate?

6. Do your words contribute to, or distract from, your intended tone?

7. Can your readers tell what your attitude is about your topic?

8. Eliminate slang, jargon, cliches, euphemisms, self-important, and emotional language.

9. Check for excessive repetition of words. Often you will catch these when reading your manuscript aloud. Be careful, however, not to remove key words in a passage. **A caution:** Rhyme is a repetition of sound, not words. And parallel construction, a fundamental of good writing, is based on repetition.

10. Circle all repeated words and consider each individually as you decide whether to keep or eliminate it.

11. Listen for slight shifts in sound and pace that one wrong word can cause.

12. Remember your audience. Are you using the correct vocabulary and length of words for them?

After carefully checking your manuscript using the guidelines in this chapter and the information in Chapter 11, "Getting Specific," you will be ready to start your search for an appropriate market.

Chapter 11:

Getting Specific

One day Judy and Laura agreed to meet for lunch. Both were on time, the restaurant was not crowded, yet they were unable to keep their luncheon date. Why? Because when Judy called Laura and made the plans, she forgot there were two Round The Clock restaurants in town. Since she did not specify which one, each girl was at a different restaurant. Good communication requires that the person speaking or writing be specific.

Check your Sentences

As you revise and rewrite, you need to check each part of your article or story to be sure it is as specific as it can be. Check your sentences. Do they answer the who, what, when, where, how, and why questions? A sentence can be grammatically correct, but not give much information.

Example:

> An offensive player scored some points.

The reader knows little about what is happening. The sentence not only does not tell how many points were scored; it does not even tell what sport was being played. And, if you really want to take it to the extreme, maybe the player was simply an obnoxious person. The sentence can be improved.

Examples:

> The fullback streaked down the field for the winning touchdown.
> The forward slam-dunked the winning basket.

Check Each Word

When you use specific instead of general words, readers can visualize the action. Some words give only a general understanding of what is happening. Choose words that express your exact meaning.

For example, *running* can refer to an Olympic sprinter *dashing* toward the finish line, or a mother *chasing* a two-year-old. Possibly, running is a batter *streaking* toward first base or a football player *racing* toward the goal line. Everyone will have a different picture. All running says is that some kind of rapid movement is happening. On the other hand, scampering brings to mind a small animal scurrying about with little steps and *lumbering* makes us think of a large animal, possibly an elephant.

As you revise, look at each word as a chance to clarify your ideas. Don't use obvious modifiers like *green* grass or blue sky. Have your grass emerald green and your sky *azure*. In addition, if you find yourself repeating the same word in a sentence or paragraph, look for appropriate synonyms.

However, you need to distinguish between useful and careless repetition. If the repetition is useful, your sentences will sound natural and logical to your reader. Parallel construction is an example of useful repetition. On the other hand, if the repetition is careless, it will annoy your readers and distract them from the idea you are presenting.

Examples:

Careless: Joan painted a *picture* of the old house, and in the *picture* she *pictured* the house as abandoned and haunted.

Better: Joan painted a picture of the old house, and in it she portrayed the house as abandoned and haunted.

Useful: The members of the team *played* with total concentration to show their devotion to their coach, and they *played* with all their energy to please their fans.

Use Active Voice

Using passive voice often weakens your sentences. The subject of a sentence in the passive voice is the object of one in the active voice. Thus, the passive voice focuses attention on the receiver rather than the doer of the action.

Example:

Passive: The ball was caught by the first baseman.

This is not an exciting sentence because it focuses attention on the ball instead of the first baseman.

Active: The first baseman caught the ball.

Now the focus is on the first baseman and creates more excitement.

In active voice, the subject names the person or thing doing the action.

Examples:

> David threw the ball. **Sally caught** it.

Using the active voice and specific action verbs makes your writing more precise. Unless you want to emphasize the receiver of the action, active voice is your best choice.

Example of when to use passive voice:

> **Active:** No one is allowed to smoke in this room.
>
> **Passive:** Smoking is not allowed in this room.

In the above case, the passive sentence is more empathic than the active since the stress is on the more important word, *smoking*.

Avoid Linking Verbs

A linking verb connects its subject with a word at or near the end of the sentence. While some linking verbs are necessary, others weaken your sentences. Often you can replace a linking verb and noun with a specific action verb related to the noun.

Example:

> **Weak:** Her remark *was an insult* to my brother.
>
> **Stronger:** Her remark *insulted* my brother.

Now the weak linking verb and noun have become a strong action verb.

The Just Right Word

Writers must carefully choose the most precise word to convey their intended meaning. When you revise, examine your writing carefully and search for general verbs like *ran, said,* or *looked*.

Replace them with vibrant, alive verbs like raced, screamed, and stared. These show readers exactly what a character is doing and capture the activity accurately.

However, verbs are not the only words to check. Search for general nouns like *vehicle, house, boy,* or *dog.* When you find them, replace them with descriptive nouns like *'66 red Ford Mustang convertible, bungalow, football quarterback,* or *Irish Setter.* Now you have created a specific image. Your reader sees the same vehicle, house, boy, and dog you do.

Next, check your adjectives and adverbs. Adjectives like *interesting, wonderful, nice,* and *cute* are vague. Only you, the writer, know for sure what you mean.

Example:
> Oscar is a *beautiful* cat.

Beautiful is vague, without details. The adjectives you choose should intensify or alter the meaning of the word they modify. Exchange vague adjectives for specific ones or give a detailed description to convey your intended meaning. In the above example, readers must take your word for it that Oscar was beautiful.

> **Better:** My cat, Oscar, has sleek, jet-black fur and a long fluffy tail.

This gives specific details and your readers see Oscar.

Adjectives and adverbs should appeal to as many of the five senses as possible. The more concrete and specific the words, the clearer the picture. For example, a cold, dark, dank dungeon is a much drearier place than a cellar or even a prison. You and your readers will be at the same restaurant and you will communicate when you choose specific words.

Figurative Language

Figurative language uses imaginative comparisons. It takes two essentially dissimilar things and finds similarities between them. Figurative language, if used carefully, can make your writing sparkle. Well-done figurative expressions make writing concrete and colorful, allowing us to put even general impressions into words. Figurative expressions appeal to readers' senses as well as to their minds. They help translate abstract ideas into unique and unforgettable pictures.

Similes and Metaphors

Instead of relying on overworked, worn-out expressions, create fresh similes and metaphors to brighten your writing.

Similes and metaphors are comparisons of two quite dissimilar things.

Similes use *like* or *as:* X is like Y.

> **Examples:** The boy leaped *like* a gazelle.
>
> …where the trunks of pines and hemlocks lay half drowned, half rotting, looking *like* alligators sleeping in the mire. [Washington Irving]
>
> As for man, his days are as grass: *as* a flower of the field, so he flourisheth. [Psalm 103:15a.]

However, *the* boy leaped like a hurdler is not a simile. *Boy* and *hurdler* are not dissimilar enough. The boy could become a hurdler. He cannot become a gazelle.

Metaphors say X is Y. To create a metaphor X becomes Y.

Examples:

> The boy *was a gazelle* as he raced for the finish line.

> The silent earthmover *was a sleeping dinosaur*.
>
> A novel *is a mirror* carried along a main road. [Stendhal]

Create interesting similes and metaphors by making a comparison between two things that are different in most ways. Well-done similes and metaphors greatly improve your writing and create images in readers' minds. They require accurate observation. The implied parallel between X and Y must fit.

Going a step farther, *a submerged metaphor* replaces X with Y. If it is effective, the reader will visualize the image and mentally fill in the comparison.

Example:

> Slowly the white wings of the boat moved against the blue cool limit of the sky. [F. Scott Fitzgerald.]

Personification

Another type of figure of speech, *personification,* gives human characteristics to nonhuman things. We see personification all the time in movies and stories: Disney's animal characters talk, and Alice meets talking animals and other nonhuman characters in *Alice in Wonderland.* Inanimate objects also can be given human characteristics. Rudyard Kipling, in his short story "The Ship That Found Herself," gives human characteristics to the parts of a ship. In *Anna and the King of Siam,* Margaret Landon personifies the dawn: "When she awoke, the dawn was climbing a low wall and creeping in through the half-opened windows."

Alliteration

Alliteration is the repetition of initial sound in two or more words. It is the most popular figure of speech. It helps people remember important points. Often, but not always, it includes the repetition of the initial letter. You can have *nervous Nellies* or *nervous knees.* In each, the initial sound is repeated.

Preachers often use alliteration to emphasize their main sermon subjects. Politicians use it so you will remember their candidate. Writers use it to help get a point across.

Political slogans:

> Victory with Vincent
>
> Progress with Pete

Travel ads:

> Come to...heavenly Hawaii
>
> ...captivating Copenhagen

Create an alliterative name for your house:

> Davies' domicile
>
> Marcia's Mansion

Who can forget the alliterative tongue-twister we all tried to say as children:

> Peter Piper picked a peck of pickled pepper; A peck of pickled pepper Peter Piper picked; Peter Piper picked a peck of pickled pepper, Where's the peck of pickled pepper Peter Piper picked?
>
> [from *Peter Piper's Practical Principles of Plain and Perfect Pronunciation, 1819*]

To be effective, alliteration, like similes and metaphors, must be fresh. Some alliterations, like "Do or die" and "Dollars to donuts" are so worn out they have become cliches. Avoid these as you would any other cliche.

Onomatopoeia

Another way to brighten your writing is by using *onomatopoeia*. When spoken, the sounds of onomatopoeic words imitate their meaning. *Buzzed, bubbling, hiss, jangle, and crackle* all sound like their meaning. You hear the *crackling* fire or the *hissing* snake ready to strike. The more of your readers' senses you can involve in your writing, the more engrossed they will be in what you have to say.

Poe was a master of onomatopoeia. He often used it to create his desired effects. In an essay, "The Philosophy of Composition," which he wrote in 1846, he detailed his search for the perfect onomatopoeic word for his classic poem "The Raven." Since he already had decided on a melancholy tone, he needed a word that would be "sonorous and susceptible of protracted emphasis . . ." His choice? The now famous "Quoth the Raven, 'Nevermore.'"

Subtle Onomatopoeia

Some onomatopoeia is more subtle, but the choice of the onomatopoeic word over the non-onomatopoeic one will add to the overall effect you want to achieve.

Examples:

> *Flash.* (The initial "fl" *flickers*.)
>
> *Jabber.* (The *-er* suffix gives the feeling of continuation.)

Other words, although not onomatopoeic, seem to reflect their meaning. For instance, *alone, lonely, loneliness,* and *emptiness* all create a sad emotion.

Oxymoron

Oxymoron is the blending of two contradictory terms. The word comes from *oxy* meaning sharp; and *moros* meaning stupid or foolish. Thus, oxymoron is a sharp-stupid saying.

Examples:

"Make *haste slowly*"

"That's a *fine mess* you've got us into this time." [Laurel and Hardy]

"Parting is such *sweet sorrow*." [Juliet in Romeo and Juliet]

Shakespeare was a master of oxymoron. In *Romeo and Juliet*, shortly after they meet and fall in love, Romeo kills Tybalt, Juliet's cousin. Juliet, madly in love with Romeo yet hating him for killing Tybalt, cries:

Beautiful tyrant, fiend angelical!

Dove-feather'd raven, wolvish-rav'ning lamb!

Despised substance of divinest show!

Just opposite to what thou justly seem'st,

A damned saint, an honorable villain!

By using oxymoron, you can make your readers sit up and think.

Synecdoche

Unlike connotations which give words added meanings, **synecdoche** lets one part stand for the whole. For example, when a teenager says he is going for a drive to show off his new "wheels," he means his new car. The wheels stand for the entire car. Likewise, the person going out to buy some new "threads" will not come home with a bag full of spools of thread, but with some new clothes. This is synecdoche.

To create synecdoche, think about what part is the most essential to the whole. Then go from there.

Metonymy

Metonymy, which is similar to synecdoche, is from the Greek word metonymia which means "substitute naming." When two things are closely connected, one may take on the properties of the other. We may say the Palace issued a statement, and everyone will know that a building hasn't suddenly started talking, but that the King or Queen has spoken. The two have been associated for so long that the Palace has taken on some of the attributes of the King or Queen.

Fabulous Realities

One way to sharpen your observer's eye is by looking for fabulous realities. Jack London in *People of the Abyss* says this about them: "The looking and discovering involved in producing fabulous realities is not a trick and not an exercise. It is the way good writers see. Because their eyes are not tired, their readers turn their pages with surprise."

A fabulous reality happens when two things that don't agree somehow come together. The touching creates numerous additional implications that are not stated. Since most people look only for the ordinary, they succeed in finding it. However, if you train yourself to daily seek "fabulous realities" you will find them everywhere. You must keep your mind open for your eyes.

Examples:

A sign in a store window: "Have your ears pierced while you wait."

Billboard: "Reese's Funeral Home

"In Hobart on Ridge Road

"24-Hour Ambulance Service

"Do something nice for your parents"

A man recently wrote a book to explain that books are now obsolete.

When you first start your search for fabulous realities, they will elude you. However, as you become accustomed to looking for the unusual, you will develop a writer's eye and will find fabulous realities all around you. Remember, the key word is *reality*. Fabulous realities must be true, not something you made up to be humorous.

Henry Thoreau put it this way: "Shams and delusions are esteemed for soundest truth, while reality is fabulous. If men would steadily observe realities only and not allow themselves to be deluded, life, to compare it with such things as we know, would be like a fairy tale and the Arabian Nights' Entertainments."

Cautions

While figurative language can brighten your writing, you should be aware that it has some weaknesses:

1. Through constant use and overuse much figurative language has been reduced to the level of a cliche and your reader will skip over it without seeing the picture or comparison you have in mind. Avoid figurative language that has become worn out by overuse.

2. If you use more than one figurative expression at a time, they should create a picture that blends into a more or less harmonious whole.

3. Be careful not to mix metaphors.

The more you practice descriptive writing, the sharper your powers of observation will become. You will begin to notice and appreciate detail that you have not seen before. Your nonwriter friends and family will not see them because they only look, they don't observe. You also will learn to discern insignificant and confusing details and cut them from your writing.

Word Connotations

As you search for fresh, alive words, you need to be aware that even though words may be synonyms, their meanings are seldom exactly the same.

For instance, if someone is *forgetful*, it carries a neutral connotation. After all, nobody's perfect, we all forget. However, if someone is *inattentive*, we feel the negative connotation immediately. It carries a feeling that the person's mind may be occupied with something else. When a person is described as *negligent*, there is an even stronger negative connotation. Negligence gives a mental image of someone deliberately forgetting. Many lawsuits are fought over negligence, so an immediate negative perception enters the mind of the reader when *negligent* is used.

In addition, *mistake, error,* and *blunder* are considered synonyms. However each has a different connotation. Several years ago during a presidential campaign, one of the candidates had done something that became a hot campaign issue. His party called it an *error;* the opposition called it a *blunder.* Each side was, of course, trying to convince voters to vote for its candidate.

If you are not aware of the connotations, you might use one with a different connotation than you really wanted.

You also need to be aware of changes in word connotations over time. For example, not many years ago if someone was *gay,* it meant he or she was a happy person. However, today *gay* has the connotation of a homosexual lifestyle.

Connotations are not only difficult to control, they are difficult to define especially when using abstract terms. Since our understanding of a word is based on personal experience, no two people will understand a word quite the same. For example, *liberal* and *con-*

servative can mean quite different things to different people. In addition, their meanings have changed over time. In his day, Thomas Jefferson was considered a political *liberal,* while in today's society, he would be considered a *conservative.* Thus, it is necessary to define what you mean when you use abstract terms. If you don't, you risk having readers respond emotionally to certain words.

Search diligently for the word that will convey your exact idea. Since connotations can manipulate the emotions of your readers, your word choice has the power to sway them to accept or reject your ideas. Readers tend to accept ideas presented in a flattering way and reject ones presented in an unflattering manner. Check word connotations very carefully because even one out-of-place "loaded" negative, or positive, connotation word could cause a reader to reject everything you've said as being biased.

Clichés

Another obstacle to clear writing is the cliché — the stereotyped, worn-out description that has become meaningless by overuse. "Slow as molasses," "in the doghouse," "hits the nail on the head," "cry over spilled milk," and "get your act together" are expressions that have been so overworked that no one pays any attention to them any more. "Where the rubber meets the road" and "bottom line" are rapidly joining the worn-out cliché ranks.

You can, however, give a cliché an unexpected twist and grab your readers' attention. In his short story, "The Daws on the Dial", James Thurber took several clichés and twisted them to suit his purpose.

Examples:

If at first you don't succeed, try, try again.

Became: If at first you don't succeed, fail, fail again.

Neither a borrower nor a lender be.

Became: Neither a burglar nor a lender be.

Because of the twists, he got a chuckle instead of a yawn from his readers.

Also, clichés become old quickly and date your writing. Since most of us want our material read for years to come, we need to avoid expressions that will soon be outdated.

Getting Specific Checklist

Use the following list as you write and revise:
1. Look for vague, generic words, phrases, and sentences. Replace them with vibrant, alive words, phrases, and sentences.
2. Be sure sentences do not leave unanswered questions.
3. Look for and remove careless word repetition.
4. Check word connotations.
5. Look for and remove cliches.
6. Create new, lively similes and metaphors.
7. When appropriate, use alliteration, oxymoron, personification, and onomatopoeic words.
8. Use the active voice whenever possible.

Now your writing will sparkle and you will not leave your reader waiting at the wrong restaurant. You will get together and communicate clearly.

EXERCISES

Choosing the Best Synonym

Check your dictionary for the exact meanings of *vast, large,* and *enormous.* Then choose which one completes the following phrases best and write it in the space provided:

1. The Mojave Desert is
2. Outer space is
3. Lake Michigan as seen from a cabin cruiser is
4. Lake Michigan as seen on a United States map is
5. Godzilla is
6. The interior of Notre Dame cathedral is

* * *

Choosing Specific Words

Replace the general word listed on the left with a specific alive one. If you can think of more than one appropriate choice, that's great!

said

The girl _____ the answer to her friend.

The angry patron _____ at the clerk.

cut

The hairdresser _____ the patron's hair.

The butcher _____ the roast.

move

The frog _____ beside the pond.

The old man _____ down the hill.

* * *

Improving Powers of Observation

This is an exercise that can help you learn to look closely at even very common objects. It will help improve your powers of observation.

Take a marshmallow and a twisted pretzel. List at least twenty-five specific details about each one. Not more than five can be ways to eat them. Use all five senses. While this may seem like an impossible assignment, it isn't.

You can use comparisons. Just be sure they, too, are as specific as you can make them. It is a good time to learn to play devil's advocate with your writing. For example, if you said, "A marshmallow is as white as snow" this could be challenged as snow that has lain for any time on a city street is not very white. But, if you said, a marshmallow is "as white as new-fallen snow," then you get an "A."

* * *

Group Activity

This exercise can help you to be more specific, but it involves at least one other person. You might want to try it in your writing group. It can be fun—and frustrating.

If you have several people, divide them into two groups and separate them either into two rooms or have them face opposite ends of the same room. A leader then displays a different object to each group. The other group is not to see or know what it is. Preferably, it is something that cannot be identified by name, such as an unusual antique or gadget of some kind.

Have each member of the group write a description of the object on a piece of paper. They should be as specific as possible, but should not call it by name if they know what it is.

After a designated time, probably ten minutes will do, the leader should remove the objects, being careful that they still have only been seen by the group writing the description.

The participants should put their names on their papers with the descriptions and then exchange them with the other group. The group that has not seen the object then tries to draw it from the descriptions given. There will be some interesting drawings.

After the drawings are completed, the papers should be returned to the ones who wrote the descriptions. If those doing the drawing had problems with the descriptions, the people who wrote the description will be able to see what was wrong with them. Such an exercise will help them learn to be more specific in their writing and avoid confusion for their readers.

* * *

Alliteration Exercise

To get your alliterative juices flowing, pick a letter—any letter—and using your brain, dictionary, and thesaurus list at least twenty words that begin with that letter. Now pick six or eight of them that sound good together. Create your own nonsense sentence tongue twister.

* * *

Creating Similes and Metaphors

Now it's time for you to create some original similes and metaphors. Don't settle for the mundane, obvious choice. Put your creative self to work and create vivid, alive images that will make your readers sit up and take notice.

1. The cluttered office is
2. The weatherbeaten oak was
3. His feet and ankles protruded out of his pants legs like
4. The silence was as thick as
5. The vultures sat expectantly on the fence like
6. The rusting car in the junkyard was
7. His harsh words cut through her like
8. The wind was
9. My heart is a
10. Time hung heavy like a

Chapter 12:

Queries That Sell

Query is short for *inquiry* and can be classified as writers' jargon. A query is a letter you write to an editor or publisher introducing yourself, suggesting an idea, and asking if her publication would be interested in seeing a complete manuscript.

Just as you cannot write a generic article or story that everyone will want to read, you cannot write a generic query letter that will fit all markets. You must slant it toward a specific publication and its readership. You must give the editor a reason why his readers will be interested.

Do not bombard the editor with ideas. Each article or story idea should be in a separate query letter. If you send more than one idea at a time, the editor will think, probably correctly, that you have not studied the markets enough to focus in on the needs of her particular publication.

Be enthusiastic about your subject. If you don't care about it, the editor isn't going to either. You have to make him care about your article or story and the people involved. Write an opening sentence that will make the editor want to read the next one. Do not start with "Do you think your readers would be interested in...?" or "Did you know that...?"

Start with something like: "Marijuana, pot, weed. These are just a few of the names for cannabis sativa, one of the most popular drugs among young people today." "While most people think of steel mills when they think of Lake County, Indiana, Lake County has much more than steel and work."

My favorite query letter opening line is one Dennis E. Hensley used in querying *Writer's Digest* about an article on Jack London. Hensley began: "How would you like an interview with a dead man?" The editor said he had to read the next line just to see how Hensley was going to do it.

Do your best writing. If you don't get a go-ahead, you won't get to write the article or story. As in the rest of your writing, use vivid words.

Tell just enough to get the editor's attention. Don't give the main point of your article or the plot of your story away.

Tell the editor why you should get the assignment. If you are writing about some problems in education and are a teacher or former teacher, your background gives you credibility. If you are discussing raising children and you have six of your own, again you have the experience to be an authority. However, if you are a carpenter and want to write about cooking for crowds, you would not have the necessary credentials, unless you and your spouse run a catering service as a sideline.

Tell what type of article it is and the sort of information that will be included. If it is a controversial issue tell her which side you are on.

Also, be sure it is the kind of writing you do and that you are interested enough in the subject to do a good job. It is difficult to write a fascinating article if you have no interest in the topic. Also, if you don't want to take the time to do the necessary research, then don't offer to write about it.

Tell the editor when you can have the manuscript ready. And whether you say it will be ready in one week or eight, have it in on time, or better yet, ahead of time. This establishes you as someone editors can count on. Many writers promise and then don't deliver. Remember, editors have deadlines, too, and if the publication isn't to the printer on time, it won't be to the readers when promised. So, if an editor is planning to use your promised article or story and you don't deliver it on time, he has to scramble to find something to take its place. This does not make a happy editor or a good relationship.

Length is important. Before telling the editor how many words you will be writing, check the publication's guidelines to see how many words they accept. Some will take 3,000; others, not more than 800.

Do not telephone editors to query unless the story is so hot that it can't wait for a letter to get to the editor. Even then, it helps if the editor has some idea ahead of time who you are. If you have written for her before, she knows your style and that you are able to write

reasonably well. If you have not yet established yourself, you are un-
likely to get a telephone assignment because she will not have any
idea what she is buying.

Be sure to address the editor by name. You will find editors'
names and titles listed in the market guides and on magazine mast-
heads.

When you send a résumé and writing samples include only one
or two samples of your *published* work. Never send copies of un-
published manuscripts. They do not prove you are a writer. Anyone
can write a manuscript and say it is an article or story. The proof is in
the publishing.

A query should be one page—two at the most and single-
spaced. Study the guidelines before writing your query. You would
not want to send a query on the benefits of nuclear energy to a publication opposed to it. Be very specific. Since the editor may want a
different slant or number of words, a query saves you the time of
writing and then doing a major rewrite to meet his specifications.

Mention the availability of photographs or other graphics. Be
sure to include your name and address and SASE. This may sound
too obvious, but some people forget to do it. At a recent writer's conference I attended, an editor mentioned that he had nine manuscripts
on his desk without names or addresses, and he doesn't have a clue
how to return them to the authors. Most editors wouldn't even care.
They would just throw them away.

If you are sending queries to non-competing markets you can
send them simultaneously. Be careful, however, if they are compet-
ing markets, because you could upset an editor if you turned him
down because you got a better offer. In either case, the first para-

graph of your query should be the sentence: "This is a simultaneous submission."

A query needs to grab the editor's interest, summarize your idea, and mention any experts you plan to use. It should show that you can organize and write simply. Even if you don't have a final title, you should include a working title. Try to make it something intriguing.

A query is not always necessary. You usually do not query on humor, editorials, newspaper articles, or anything else shorter than 1,000 words. With short material, the editor can evaluate the manuscript in the same time as a query. With humor, there is no way an editor can tell whether or not you are going to be funny throughout the manuscript without reading your story.

Just as with your manuscript, be sure your query is error-free. Check and double check your grammar, punctuation, and spelling. Remember, first impressions are lasting ones. Make yours a good one.

Chapter 13:

Marketing Your Manuscript

You now have your article or story written and revised. It's time to get it ready to send to an editor. However, before stuffing it into an envelope and waving goodbye, you have more work to do. Sorry about that.

Preparing the Manuscript

The first thing to do is to make the text is as perfect as possible. Check carefully for errors. It is easy to read what you *think* is on the paper and not catch a misspelled word or an inverted one (*saw* for *was,* for example). While a computer's spell checker will detect misspelled words, it *cannot* detect a correctly spelled wrong one. Ideally, a friend or relative who is a good proofreader can go over your manuscript for you. However, most of us have to do the job ourselves.

Manuscript errors cause you to lose credibility with editors. Editors are trained to spot errors and will think you are careless if they find any in your manuscript. I once heard of an editor rejecting a manuscript because the writer spelled one word wrong. The writer had submitted an article about food poisoning and had misspelled ptomaine by leaving off the "p". The editor reasoned that if she was careless about spelling that important a word that she may have been careless in her research as well. Logically, the editor didn't want to take a chance on the article, and a possible lawsuit if someone got sick.

Read your manuscript aloud. It is amazing the mistakes you find this way. Not only will this help you locate word errors, but will let you hear how your manuscript will sound to your readers. You may find a sentence that looks great on paper but does not sound so wonderful when read out loud. You also can discover places where you have repeated a word often and need to use some synonyms. I caught myself using catch throughout this paragraph, so checked the thesaurus for some synonyms.

Do a line-by-line check for spelling errors. The best technique is to take a ruler and place it under each line as you read the manuscript. While slow, the process is rewarding. Some people suggest reading your manuscript backwards to locate spelling errors as you will be concentrating on each individual word since the writing will not make sense. This method will work for actual spelling errors but will not spot inverted words.

Once you have all the bugs out, you need to type your manuscript in a proper form. For example of proper manuscript form, see page 192. Be sure to use good quality white nonerasable paper. Erasable paper will smear if it gets damp. It's a fact of life that editors often read manuscripts with a coffee cup in one hand and your manuscript in the other. If some coffee should accidentally spill on your manuscript, you still want it to be legible. Erasable paper also can smear just from being handled, another reason to avoid it. Preferred is 20# bond; 16# will pass.

Be sure your typewriter keys are clean and use a fresh, black ribbon. Use pica (preferred) or elite type. Do not use script or other fancy types because they are difficult to read. If you use a computer, the same rules apply. You should use standard type, a new black ribbon and printing should be letter quality. Although its quality is getting better, dot matrix is harder to read and many editors will not even read a manuscript printed with dot matrix.

Remember, editors read for hours at a time. They do not appreciate hard-to-read manuscripts. Do everything you can to make their job easier. This also will give them a more favorable first impression of your submission.

Type on one side of the paper only. Leave ample (1 - 1½") margins on all sides. If your typewriter has pica type, you can use one inch margins; if it has elite type, use one and one-half inch ones. This gives editors some place to make notations. The entire manuscript, including long quotations that are indented, should be double spaced.

Keep correction tape or white out correction fluid available for those inevitable typing mistakes. It is acceptable to make up to two or three *minor* corrections per page in black ink. Any more than that will look sloppy and you should retype the page. If you use a computer or word processor, you should have no ink corrections on the page. If you find an error, you should correct it and run out another copy of that page.

Never send an editor a handwritten manuscript. If you don't know how to type, hire someone to type your final draft. Most writer's magazines include classified ads by people wanting to type manuscripts. If you live near a college, some students always are looking for typing jobs to earn a little extra spending money.

The manuscript should be held together with a #1 regular silver colored metal paper clip. Do not use fancy or plastic ones. DO NOT staple your manuscript. Editors want to be able to take it apart easily.

Estimating Number of Words

To estimate the number of words in a manuscript of less than twenty-five pages, count the number of words on the first three pages, divide by three and multiply the result by the total number of pages in the manuscript. For example, if page 1 has 150 words, page 2 has 245 words, and page 3 has 260, you have a total of 655 or an average of 218 per page. Then, multiply 218 times the number of manuscript pages; for example 218 x 8 = 1,744 words. If the manuscript is over twenty-five pages, use the same procedure, except you take an average of the first five pages. After you have your estimated word count, round it to the nearest twenty-five. For example, both 1,221 and 1,234 would become approximately 1,225.

While some word processing programs do a word count, they are not always accurate. I know the word count I get with mine tends to be a little high. I'm not sure why. I think it may be counting the words in the headers, footers, and footnotes in addition to the actual text.

Choosing Markets

When deciding which publishers to submit to, you need to find out what word count they will accept. Most publications have guidelines that tell the number of words they want for specific types of writing. It is a waste of time and postage to send a 2,500-word article or story to a publication whose longest articles and stories are 1,200 words. That oversight will get you an immediate rejection. This also will tell the editor you have not taken the time necessary to become familiar with the publication or to read the guidelines.

Most publications supply guidelines free for a business size SASE (self-addressed, stamped envelope). Some also supply sample copies of their publication free, while others charge for them. If the publication is not available on the newsstand, you will want to send for a sample copy so you can see what kinds of articles and stories it wants, how it is laid out, and get an idea of its audience. You can learn about the audience by reading the ads, editorials, and letters to the editor. Also, look at the cover. Whom does it appeal to? You'll want to start an alphabetical file of sample copies and guidelines so you can find them quickly when you need them.

In addition, when writing for inspirational markets you need to know what version of the Bible the publication uses. Some use the King James Version (KJV), while others use the New International Version (NIV) or another modern language version. Also, some want the biblical quotation written out while others prefer that you paraphrase the verse or verses and mention where it is found.

Copyright Protection

You want to be sure your material is copyrighted when you sell it. Otherwise anyone is free to take it verbatim and call it their own. Not nice, but not illegal. Most publications copyright the entire publication, so there is no problem. A few of the smaller publications do not. This fact is usually mentioned in *Writer's Market* and on the masthead of the publication. If you sell to a publication that is not copyrighted, ask the editor to include the copyright symbol and your name under the title of your article or story.

Know the Editor

After you decide where to send your manuscript, look in the latest *Writer's Market* guide for the editor's name. If an editor and a managing editor are listed and no preference is designated, send your manuscript to the managing editor. That person probably has more time to look at it than the editor and can pass your manuscript on to the editor if it looks promising. If the magazine designates a specific editor it wants manuscripts and queries sent to, by all means send yours to that editor.

Editors at some publications change so often they seem to be playing musical chairs. However, they expect you, the writer, to keep up with them. To help keep you informed, most writer's magazines have columns in each issue devoted to that information.

If the magazine is on the newsstand, you can check the masthead of the current issue for any editorial changes. And, just to be on the safe side, you always can call the magazine and ask whomever answers the telephone if Jane Jones is still managing editor. The call shouldn't take more than a minute and can be well worth the twenty-five cents or so it costs if there has been an editorial change and you didn't know about it.

The Cover Letter

Now you are ready to sell your product to an editor. While an editor can figure out that you have sent your manuscript hoping to have it published, always send a cover letter along with it.

A cover letter should be brief, not more than one page single spaced. Although you double space your manuscript, single space the cover letter in your choice of accepted letter formats. Avoid starting paragraphs with "I." You want the focus to be on your material, not on you.

Like the first paragraph of your manuscript, the first paragraph of the cover letter should grab the editor's attention. State a startling or interesting fact contained in your article. Or give some of the drama of your story, but don't tell the ending. You want them to want to read your manuscript to find out what happened. Show the editor why your manuscript will interest his readers. DO NOT tell him it will sell lots of copies and all your friends and relatives will be sure to buy it. He will decide whether it will help sell copies.

The second paragraph can mention the article or story's name, what rights you are offering, and if you are sending photographs with the manuscript. Including usable photographs greatly increases your chances of sale because you are saving busy editors from having to find some to go with the article. You also usually get extra money for any pictures they use.

In the third paragraph, you can mention any writing credits you have. If you have credits, mention those in publications similar to the one to which you are sending your manuscript. For example, I do quite a bit of writing for the inspirational market, and if I send a manuscript to a publication I have not sold to before, I will include any sales to other publications within the same denomination. Otherwise, I mention two or three of the better-known publications in the inspirational field that have purchased my material. Or, if I am submitting an article on writing, I will mention other writer's magazines that have published my articles. Once you have sold to a publication, however, it is not necessary to keep telling the editor you have been published elsewhere when submitting future manuscripts.

If you do not yet have any writing credits, just leave this paragraph out. DO NOT mention that you have not yet been published.

If your manuscript concerns a topic that should be written by someone who *knows* what they are talking about, tell the editor why you are qualified to write it. For example, if you are writing an article about the problems of dealing with a hyperactive child, you either should be the parent of or a trained professional who works with this type of child on a regular basis. Editors are not going to be interested in hearing your thoughts on the problem if your main contact with hyperactive children is seeing them misbehave in grocery stores.

The final paragraph should mention that you are enclosing a self-addressed, stamped envelope (SASE) for the editor's convenient response. The SASE is a MUST. Without it you will not see your manuscript again. Editors receive hundreds and sometimes thousands of unsolicited manuscripts a month and there is no reason they can, or should, pay the return postage.

If you are sending your manuscript in response to an editor's positive response to your query letter (see chapter 12, writing query letters), mention this in your cover letter. You also may want to enclose a photocopy of the editor's actual go ahead. Since it is now requested material, write this on the envelope. Type "Requested Material" on the left hand side of the envelope approximately one to two inches below your return address. Doing so will alert editors that this envelope is one they are expecting and your manuscript will get priority handling. It will not go into the slush pile of unsolicited manuscripts that they get around to when they can.

While letterheads are not mandatory, they help give the impression that you are a professional writer. Letterheads should be printed on good quality bond paper. All the information you need to include is your name, address, and telephone number. You do not need to put on them that you are a freelance writer. Have the letterheads printed on either white or off-white paper. No fancy colors, please. This immediately labels you AMATEUR.

Pictures with Articles

A black and white picture should be printed on glossy paper and be at least 5" x 7" and preferably 8 ½" x 11". Do not write on the back, because this will damage the picture. You can write any identifying information, such as name or file number, on labels and stick them to the back of the picture.

Color slides should be 35mm or larger. Be sure to send color *slides,* not color prints. Because exposure to light will eventually cause slides to fade, get duplicate slides made and send them instead of your originals. In addition to preserving your irreplaceable slides, duplicates save the trauma of lose or damage to your original slides. Keep your originals safely filed in a dark, dry place.

When you have people pose for a photograph, it is a good idea to get them to sign a model release stating that you have permission to use the picture for publication. This protects you and the publication you sell the picture to if they later decide they wish they had not posed for it. Also, if you are planning to use the photograph to endorse something or someone, always obtain a model release from anyone who poses for the pictures. (See sample on page 191.)

When mailing photographs, you need to do several things. Label each slide or black and white picture with your name, an identifying number, and the name of the person who took the picture if you didn't. I cut the edges off self-sticking return address labels so they will fit on a side of the slide and use them to identify the slides with my name. Also, include a list of captions and identify any recognizable people in the pictures.

Put color slides in plastic sheets which are available at camera shops. If you only are sending two or three you may want to cut the page so that you have just the size you need.

If I send just one or two black and white pictures with an article I put them inside picture folders. However, it is quite acceptable to put them between two pieces of cardboard. If I send several, I cut thin paper, such as onion skin or waxed paper, to size and place a sheet between pictures so they won't stick together if it should get humid.

Clearly mark the envelope and your SASE: "Contains Photos, Do Not Bend." If you are going to be continually sending out manuscripts with pictures, you may want to have a rubber stamp made that says, "Contains Photos, Do Not Bend." Rubber stamps are not expensive and can save time. Stamped information and labels also give your envelopes a professional look.

Mailing the Manuscript

As first class postage rates continue to climb, you will be tempted to send your manuscript by fourth class book rate. While fourth class is cheaper, it takes longer and may give the editor a message that you don't think enough of your manuscript to use first class. In addition, undelivered first class mail is returned to sender, while undelivered fourth class goes in the post office's circular file. So, using first class also will guarantee that if your manuscript cannot be delivered it will be returned to you. You won't be left wondering what happened to it.

Money Saving Tip: There is a slight decrease in the cost of first class postage after the first ounce, for letters weighing more than one ounce. As you begin sending out more and more manuscripts, this little extra savings can become a considerable amount over a year's time. And, on heavier manuscripts, priority mail is another money saver. It gets first class treatment but costs less. Priority mail can weigh as much as seventy pounds, but packages weighing up to two pounds are all the same price. Check with your post office for current rates. Since postage is tax deductible, always get a receipt when you buy stamps or send out book manuscripts.

The high cost of postage is an additional incentive to study the markets carefully. Doing your marketing homework can help avoid sending your manuscript to an editor who has no interest in your topic, or who recently may have published a similar article or story.

Testing the market first with a query letter can also save you postage because a one-page query is much less expensive to send than a complete manuscript. Again, however, check the market guides. Some publications will accept either a query or a complete manuscript, others will only accept a query, and still others only the complete manuscript.

If your manuscript is three pages or less you can tri-fold it and put it in a #10 business size (9 ½" x 4 ¼") envelope. You, of course, also will tri-fold your SASE before adding it to the envelope. The business envelope saves postage over a heavier manuscript envelope. While the business envelope usually weighs over an ounce, needing two stamps, when you send it out, it comes back weighing an ounce or less and needing only one stamp. On the other hand, postal regulations require extra postage on all larger envelopes weighing less than one ounce. Again, check with your post office for current rate.

Longer manuscripts should be mailed flat in a 9x12 or 10x13 inch first class envelope. If your manuscript is too thick for a regular 9 x12 or 10x13first class envelope, you can purchase large padded envelopes for manuscripts of up to one hundred pages. You, of course, include the same type of envelope for your SASE. Any much longer than that should be mailed flat, without paper clips, in a letter size box. Special manuscript boxes come in a variety of depths for different lengths of manuscripts. Some also are sized so one fits directly inside another, with the inside one becoming your SASE. Or you can mail your manuscript in a paper box. If you are sending your manuscript in a paper box, mark it "Save for return." Be sure to include a return address label with your name and address already typed on it and sufficient stamps or a check for postage.

Canadian Markets

Don't overlook Canadian markets. However, postage to Canada is slightly higher than to destinations within the United States. Check with your local post office for the current rates. Also, don't send them an SASE with United States postage attached; they cannot use it. When sending to Canadian markets, you either can send an SASE with Canadian postage attached (available through the Canadian postal service), or you can use International Reply Coupons (IRC's), available at United States post offices. IRC's are quite expensive and you need one for each ounce. You can save money by photocopying your manuscript and requesting that the editor only return an acceptance or rejection, which only needs one IRC.

No Gimmicks, Please

Do not use gimmicks when sending out your manuscript. Holly Miller, former senior editor of *The Saturday Evening Post,* tells of a writer who spray painted her envelopes with gold paint to attract the editors' attention. However, the only extra attention she received was to have her manuscripts put on the bottom of the slush pile because no one wanted the sticky paint on her hands and possibly on her clothes.

Keep a Copy

Just as you should never, never, never feed gremlins after midnight, you should never, never, never send out your only copy of your manuscript. It can get lost. Somehow, you can never recreate exactly what you have written.

Editors get stacks of mail, most of which is unsolicited. While it doesn't happen often, occasionally manuscripts do get lost. Also, I read somewhere, although I am sure they will hotly deny it, that the post office is unable to deliver approximately ten percent of the mail.

Several years ago I had a manuscript lost. I don't know who lost the manuscript and it really doesn't matter. Fortunately I had a back-up copy, so I typed up a fresh manuscript to send back to the publication. The editor did buy the piece and put it into pamphlet form. Since then, the story has been published in two anthologies. If I hadn't had my copy, I am sure I would not have been able to duplicate the story, and I'm not sure I would have taken the time and effort to try to rewrite the manuscript.

Follow-Up

In most cases, you can expect to wait several weeks for a response to a manuscript submission. Again, your market guide usually will tell you how long you can expect to wait. Remember, you are dealing with very busy people; yours is *not* the only manuscript they are reading. However, if you have waited the time indicated in their guidelines or the market guide, and have given them an extra month for good measure, you can drop a *friendly* note inquiring about the manuscript's status. The manuscript may have gotten misplaced, still may be under consideration, or the post office may never have delivered it. If the manuscript has gotten lost and you still are interested in that particular publication, offer to send them another copy.

Keeping Track of Manuscripts

When you first start writing, you will only have a few manuscripts out and it is not difficult to keep track of them. However, if you are a serious writer, before long you will need a system to record where they are, how long they have been out, where they have been—and where they will go next. All writers have slightly different ways of monitoring manuscripts. Here's what works for me. You can decide what will work best for you.

Each time I send out a manuscript, I write the date, the publication I sent it to, and the article name, in a stenographer's notebook. As the manuscript is sold or returned, I note its progress beside its name. Since this list is in chronological order, I can easily flip through and see if any have been away too long.

I also have a file folder for each article or query and keep these separate from my other files. In fact, my work area is so arranged that I have a two-drawer file cabinet containing my working files next to the desk my computer and typewriter are on. Keeping my files close by is convenient when I work on the marketing aspect of my business. You will find that marketing will take a big bite out of your writing time, so anything you can do to streamline it will give you a few extra minutes to create.

On the inside front of the file folder, I keep a running list with dates of submission, publisher submitted to, and name of the article or story. I also have a Post-it™ note attached with three or four markets where it can be sent should it return home with a rejection slip attached.

In this folder I keep a copy of the letter I sent to the editor. All I have to do is retype it, addressed to the new editor. Actually, I put it through my word processing program, which is faster, since all I have to do is change the date and inside address.

Also, on the inside front cover of the file folder I make a note of what publications have purchased the manuscript and what rights they bought. When a publication buys first rights, you cannot send it to another publication until after it has been published. Once it has been published, however, you are free to resell it.

Don't let rejection get you down. The best way to do this is to get the manuscript out of its SASE and back out to another editor the same day it comes home. If you are going to be a successful writer, you don't have time for pity parties. Remember, you as a person are not being rejected. It is just that they cannot use your manuscript *at the present time.* This remailing goes much faster if you already have done your homework and have additional markets in mind. Remember my Post-it™ note?

As each editor has his particular likes and dislikes, keep track of who was at a particular publication when you made your submission. Then, when he or she moves on, you may want to try that publication again, if you are sure your article or story is targeted for that market.

Also, once you have started selling to a particular publication and the editor moves to another one, it can be easier to break into that new market because the editor is already familiar with you. She likes your style or she wouldn't have been buying your manuscripts. If she has moved to a publication you are interested in writing for, try her there.

RIGHTS TO SELL

First North American Serial Rights

First North American Serial Rights entitle the publisher to be the first periodical to publish your article or story in the United States and/or Canada. Once it has been published, you can resell *one-time* or *reprint* rights as many times as you can find buyers.

Reprint Rights

When you submit your manuscript after it has been published the first time, you offer "Reprint" or "Second" rights. Again, you need to do your homework. Some publications only accept first rights, so do not waste your time and postage sending them something that has been published elsewhere. *Reprint* rights is interchangable with *second* rights. Even if you are selling a story for the fifth time, you are still selling second (or reprint) rights.

One-Time Rights

Some publications will purchase "one-time" rights, which differ from "first rights." With one-time rights, the publisher is buying the right to use your article or story one time, but not necessarily the first time. Unlike "first rights," which require you to wait to submit your manuscript to another publisher until after it has been published, after the purchase of one-time rights you are free to submit it to other nonoverlapping publications. For these future submissions you would also label rights offered "one- time."

Once I have sold first rights and the article or story has been published, I put "one-time" on my manuscripts. At this point there is not much difference between "one-time" and "reprint" and I guess it goes back to word connotations—I just think "one- time" sounds better.

All Rights

Some publications buy "all rights." This means exactly what it says. They now own the manuscript and you no longer have any rights to it. After they have published it, you can request that reprint rights be returned to you, but they are not required to do so. In the beginning it may be necessary to sell all rights to get some writing credits, but after you have established yourself, do not do so unless it is to a high paying, prestigious market.

Helpful Hints

When you get the complimentary copy of the magazine containing your article or story, compare it with your copy of the manuscript. There usually will be a few fine-tuning changes that will improve it. Be sure to incorporate these before sending your manuscript out again.

Once you start selling regularly to a variety of publications, keep a list of the publications and the articles or stories each has purchased. Along with the notes inside your file folder, this sold-to list will keep you from submitting something they have already purchased. Such a situation usually does not become a concern until you start selling one-time rights of the same article or story to several different publications.

Also, if you write several similar articles on the same topic, you may not want to submit the others to a publication that has already bought one of them. This sold-to list can help you there, as your file folder notes will not contain this information. I keep my sold-to list on 3x5 cards. For example, I write quite a few articles on the various drugs of abuse. Some are slanted to the teen market and others to the adult. In addition, I may write two dealing with slightly different aspects of the same drug, such as tobacco, and I do not want to send another article on tobacco to a publication that has already purchased one.

Now your manuscript is in letter perfect form and your marketing research is done. Go out there and sell, sell, sell.

Model Release

In consideration for value received, receipt whereof is acknowledged, I hereby give (your name) the absolute right and permission to copyright and/or publish, and/or resell photographic portraits or pictures of me, or in which I may be included in whole or in part, for art, advertising, trade or any other lawful purpose whatsoever.

I hereby waive any right that I may have to inspect and/or approve the finished product or the advertising copy that may be used in connection therewith, or the use to which it may be applied.

I hereby release, discharge and agree to save the publisher from any liability by virtue of any blurring, distortion, alteration, optical illusion or use in composite form, whether intentional or otherwise, that may occur or be produced in the making of said pictures, or in any processing tending toward the completion of the finished product.

Date _____   Model_____

                                   Address _____

                                     _____

Witness _____

[from *Writing For Profit* by Dennis E. Hensley. Used by permission]

Sample Manuscript

Your legal name   ©199___ by (your legal name)
Mailing address   Fiction or Nonfiction
City, State, Zip Code   Rights Offered:
Telephone number, incl. area code   Approximate number of words
 Social Security Number

Title of article or story

by: name you want used (legal or pen name)

Double or triple space down and start writing. Indent five
spaces at beginning of each paragraph.

....

Second and following pages:

Name   Page number   Identifying word
                                                              or words (all on one line)

Space down three spaces and continue typing.

Chapter 14:

Grammar Revisited

It is time to consider one of the more technical parts of writing. Unfortunately, many high school and some college students do not see the importance in speaking and writing correctly. Their only concern is being understood. You *know* what I mean. They don't seem to understand that correct grammar contributes to clear under-standing. And as Robert Lewis Stevenson said, "Don't write merely to be understood. Write so that you cannot possibly be misunderstood."

As writers, it is essential that we use good grammar. Not only do editors look unfavorably on manuscripts full of errors, but if we succumb to poor grammar usage, the quality of standard English will continue to slip.

This chapter will give you a quick review of your high school grammar class as painlessly as possible.

Subject/Verb Agreement

The first area to consider is subject/verb agreement. One general rule governs this: A subject and its verb <u>must</u> agree in number.

That is, simply, if the subject is singular (refers to one person, place, thing, or idea) then the verb must be singular. Conversely, if the subject is plural (refers to two or more persons, places, things, or ideas) then the verb must be plural. Most of the time, the choice is simple, and our ear often will tell us what is correct and incorrect.

You should have no difficulty recognizing singular and plural forms of nouns. <u>Most</u> singular nouns do not have an -*s* or -*es* on the end: star, car, box. With the exception of irregular nouns like *man/men* and *mouse/mice,* plural nouns have an -*s* or -*es* on the end: stars, cars, boxes.

Personal pronouns, words that take the place of a noun or nouns, also are either singular or plural.

Personal Pronouns

	Singular	Plural
First Person:	I, me, my, mine	we, us, our, ours
Second Person:	you, your, yours	you, your, yours
Third Person:	he, him, his, she her, hers,	they, them, their, it, its, theirs

However, what's challenging about correct usage of the English language is its inconsistency. Rarely will you find a rule of grammar with the word *always* in it. As soon as you look at the chart showing singular and plural pronouns and decide it's easy enough, I have to bring up an exception: The second person *you* uses a plural verb and *sometimes* the first person singular does too.

Example:

You *are* wanted on the telephone.

I *have* been working a puzzle.

The good news is that third person singular pronouns always use a singular verb. Of course, the plural forms of all three persons use the plural verb. (Don't blame me, I didn't make up the rules.)

Verbs

Like nouns and pronouns, verbs have number. Two problem areas are number in the simple present tense, (*I laugh, he laughs,*) and in tenses using a form of be (including *is, are, was, were*) as a helping verb.

While an -*s* or -*es* on a noun makes it plural, adding an -s or -es to a verb makes it singular. In fact, this is one of the few places in a grammar book you will find *always* used.

When a form of *be* is used as a helping verb, it often will indicate whether a verb phrase is singular or plural.

Forms of <u>Be</u>

am	am being	can be	have been
are	are being	could be	has been
is	is being	may be	had been
was	was being	might be	could have been

were	were being	must be	may have been
		shall be	might have been
		should be	must have been
		will be	shall have been
		would be	should have been
			will have been
			would have been

The above chart includes examples of *be* verbs in the present, past, and present perfect tenses. Since these are the only forms of *be* that change form from singular to plural, they are the ones that cause agreement problems.

Examples of singular subject and verb:

John always rides his bike to school.

She is ready to go shopping.

Robin was doing her homework.

I am reading *Moby Dick*.

Examples of plural subject and verb:

The Jones boys always ride their bikes to school.

They are ready to go shopping.

The children were doing their homework.

We are reading *Moby Dick*.

Since the verb is close to the subject in all of the above sentences, they cause little problem. However, when a phrase or clause is added between the subject and its verb, we may forget what the subject is and have the verb agree with a noun or pronoun in the phrase or clause that separates them. Keep in mind that a phrase or clause between the subject and its verb does not affect subject/verb agreement.

Example:

> One of the boys is going.

One is the subject and is singular. *Of the boys* is a prepositional phrase explaining who *one* is. Thus, the singular *one* takes the singular verb *is*. Don't be fooled by the plural *boys* next to the verb; it is not the subject. The subject of a sentence will never be found in a prepositional phrase.

Example:

> The boys from our town are planning a party.

Since boys is the subject and is plural, it takes the plural verb *are*. *From our town* gives information about *boys*.

Sometimes the phrase or clause separating the subject and verb is even more lengthy and it takes more effort to determine which word is actually the subject.

> My friend who has been on a round-the-world cruise for several months has finally returned. (The singular subject *friend* takes the singular has.
>
> The boys most likely to win the competition are Steve and Tom. (The plural subject boys takes the plural are.)

Hint: The subject of an active sentence will be the person or thing doing the action. So, if you find the verb, see what the action is and then identify who or what is doing it. When you do, you usually will have your subject.

Tenses

A *tense* is a form of a verb that shows time of action or state of being. English verbs use six tenses. Three are simple: present, past, and future; and three are perfect: present perfect, past perfect, and future perfect.

Each of the six tenses has two forms: *basic* and *progressive.* A third form, the *emphatic,* occurs only in the present and past tenses.

The Basic, Progressive, and Emphatic Forms
of the Six Tenses

Tense	Basic Form	Progressive Form	Emphatic Form
Present	use	am using	do use
Past	used	was using	did use
Future	will use	will be using	
Present Perf	haveused	have been using	
Past Perfect	had used	had been using	
Future Perf	will have used	will have been using	

A verb has four principal parts: the present (base form), the present participle, the past, and the past participle. The past and past participles of a regular verb are formed by adding -ed or -d to the present form.

Examples:

worked smiled

The past and past participles of irregular verbs are not formed by adding -ed or -d. The following is a list of most irregular verbs and their forms:

IRREGULAR VERB FORMS

Present	Present Participle	Past	Past Participle
arise	arising	arose	(have) arisen
awake	awaking	awoke	(have) awaken
bear	bearing	bore	(have) borne

beat	beating	beaten or beat	(have) beaten or beat
begin	beginning	began	(have) begun
bend	bending	bent	(have) bent
bid	bidding	bid	(have) bid
bind	binding	bound	(have) bound
blow	blowing	blew	(have) blown
break	breaking	broke	(have) broken
bring	bringing	brought	(have) brought
build	building	built	(have) built
burst	bursting	burst	(have) burst
buy	buying	bought	(have) bought
catch	catching	caught	(have) caught
choose	choosing	chose	(have) chosen
cling	clinging	clung	(have) clung
come	coming	came	(have) come
creep	creeping	crept	(have) crept
cut	cutting	cut	(have) cut
dig	digging	dug	(have) dug
do	doing	did	(have) done
draw	drawing	drew	(have) drawn
drink	drinking	drank	(have) drunk
drive	driving	drove	(have) driven
eat	eating	ate	(have) eaten
fall	falling	fell	(have) fallen
fight	fighting	fought	(have) fought
find	finding	found	(have) found
fling	flinging	flung	(have) flung
fly	flying	flew	(have) flown
forget	forgetting	forgot	(have) forgotten
forsake	forsaking	forsook	(have) forsaken
freeze	freezing	froze	(have) frozen
get	getting	got	(have) got or gotten

give	giving	gave	(have) given
go	going	went	(have) gone
grind	grinding	ground	(have) ground
grow	growing	grew	(have) grown
hang (to kill)	hanging	hanged	(have) hanged
hang	hanging	hung	(have) hung
hide	hiding	hid	(have) hidden
hit	hitting	hit	(have) hit
hold	holding	held	(have) held
hurt	hurting	hurt	(have) hurt
keep	keeping	kept	(have) kept
know	knowing	knew	(have) known
lay	laying	laid	(have) laid
lead	leading	led	(have) led
leave	leaving	left	(have) left
lend	lending	lent	(have) lent
let	letting	let	(have) let
lie	lying	lay	(have) lain
lose	losing	lost	(have) lost
mean	meaning	meant	(have) meant
pay	paying	paid	(have) paid
put	putting	put	(have) put
ride	riding	rode	(have) ridden
ring	ringing	rang	(have) rung
rise	rising	rose	(have) risen
run	running	ran	(have) run
say	saying	said	(have) said
see	seeing	saw	(have) seen
sell	selling	sold	(have) sold
send	sending	sent	(have) sent
set	setting	set	(have) set
shake	shaking	shook	(have) shaken

shine	shining	shone/shined	(have) shone/shined
shoot	shooting	shot	(have) shot
show	showing	showed	(have) showed or shown
shrink	shrinking	shrank	(have) shrunk
shut	shutting	shut	(have) shut
sing	singing	sang	(have) sung
sink	sinking	sank	(have) sunk
sit	sitting	sat	(have) sat
slay	slaying	slew	(have) slain
sleep	sleeping	slept	(have) slept
speak	speaking	spoke	(have) spoken
spend	spending	spent	(have) spent
spin	spinning	spun	(have) spun
split	splitting	split	(have) split
spread	spreading	spread	(have) spread
spring	springing	sprang	(have) sprung
stand	standing	stood	(have) stood
steal	stealing	stole	(have) stolen
stick	sticking	stuck	(have) stuck
sting	stinging	stung	(have) stung
stride	striding	strode	(have) stridden
strike	striking	struck	(have) struck
strive	striving	strove	(have) striven
swear	swearing	swore	(have) sworn
swim	swimming	swam	(have) swum
swing	swinging	swung	(have) swung
take	taking	took	(have) taken
teach	teaching	taught	(have) taught
tear	tearing	tore	(have) torn
throw	throwing	threw	(have) thrown
thrust	thrusting	thrust	(have) thrust
tread	treading	trod	(have) trodden

wear	wearing	wore	(have) worn
weave	weaving	wove	(have) woven
			or wove
win	winning	won	(have) won
wind	winding	wound	(have) wound
wring	wringing	wrung	(have) wrung
write	writing	wrote	(have) written

The three forms of the present tense can be used to show present actions or conditions as well as various continuous actions or conditions.

EXAMPLES OF VERB TENSE

Present

Simple Perfect

Present action: There they *are.*
Present condition: The humidity *is* very high today.
Regularly occurring action: Mother *shops* on Tuesdays.
Regularly occurring condition: The leaves *are* colorful in the fall.
Constant action: The sun *rises* in the east.
Constant condition: The heart *is* a muscle.

Present Progressive

Long continuing action: Leah *is taking* piano lessons.
Short continuing action: Jerome *is singing* "The Holy City."
Continuing action: Since his accident, John *is being* more careful.

Present Emphatic

Emphasizing a statement: I *do think* you did it.

Denying a contrary assertion: Contrary to popular opinion, the mayor *is doing* a good job.

Past

Simple Past

Completed action: Henry *completed* the assignment.

Condition no longer existing: Sam *was* tired after running ten miles.

Past Progressive

Long continuing action in the past: My Aunt Olive *was making* quilt blocks last winter.

Short continuing action in the past: Jerome *was singing* "The Holy City" when the lights went out.

Continuing condition in the past: Linda *was being* truthful about the accident.

Past Emphatic

Emphasizing a statement: I *did enjoy* her friendship until recently.

Denying a contrary assertion: But I *did read* the assignment.

Present Perfect

Completed action (indefinite time): Olive *has finished* the quilt.

Completed condition (indefinite time): Wayne *has been* here, too.

Action continuing to present: She *has taught* here for five years.

Condition continuing to present: They *have been* here since 1987.

Present Perfect Progressive

Past action continuing to the present: Jerry *has been reading War and Peace.*

Past Perfect

Action completed before another past action: She *had taught* here for five years before moving to Chicago.

Condition completed before another past condition: John *had been* a teacher for ten years before Renee was.

Past Perfect Progressive

Past action continuing from indefinite to definite time: The crops in Nevada *had been flourishing* until the hordes of crickets descended from the mountains.

Future

Simple Future

Action in the future: They *will go* home tomorrow.

Condition in the future: The clothes *will be* dry in ten minutes.

Future Progressive

Continuous action in the future: The classes *will be meeting* during October and November.

Future Perfect

Future action completed before another: Before you go home he *will have finished* restoring his antique car.

Future condition completed before another: Her brother *will have been* out of high school for two years before she enters as a freshman.

Future Perfect Progressive

Continuous action completed before another future action begins: By the time she moves to Chicago in June, she *will have been teaching* for more than five years.

Question: When is a Verb Not a Verb?

Answer: When it's a verbal.

Gerunds, participles, and infinitives are derived from verbs and are therefore called *verbals*.

Gerunds

Sometimes a verb functions as a noun and then it is called a *gerund*. (I know you're really going to enjoy this.) Many nouns that end in *-ing* are actually verbals. Actually, gerunds are not hard to recognize if you will remember they <u>always</u> end in *-ing* and <u>always</u> function as nouns. (Isn't that exciting—two *always* in the same grammar rule!)

Here are some ways you may be using gerunds as nouns without realizing it.

Examples:

As a subject: *Jogging* is my favorite pastime.

As a direct object: He put a new *binding* on the book.

As an indirect object: Her extravagance gave *spending* a new meaning.

As an object of preposition: Susan enjoys the pastime of *swimming*.

As a predicate nominative: Joan's favorite hobby is *sewing*.

As an appositive: Joan's favorite hobby, *sewing*, occupies much of her time.

Participles

Now that we have determined that gerunds always end in *-ing* you think it's safe to say that every time you see a verb ending in *-ing* that isn't acting as a verb then it is a gerund. WRONG. It may be a *participle*. If it is a participle it will always function as an adjective. Well, at least that's encouraging. If you keep these distinctions in mind, participles won't be as bad as they seem.

Examples

Verb: Fred is *running*.

Gerund: *Running* is good exercise.

Participle: The *running* boy almost tripped.

Infinitives

Now we come to the third and final kind of verbal—the infinitive. An *infinitive* verbal form follows the word *to* and acts as a noun, adjective, or adverb. They will be easier to identify if you remember they always follow the word to.

Infinitives can act as nouns in almost as many ways as gerunds can.

Infinitives As Nouns

Subject: *To begin* can be half done.

Direct object: Getting home late, Murray hoped *to sleep*.

Predicate nominative: The bird's only chance of escape was *to fly*.

Object of Preposition: Poised on the board, Jan was about *to dive*.

Appositive: Murray's desire, *to sleep,* was interrupted by the ringing of the telephone.

Infinitive As Adjective

His experiment propagated one of the first bacteria *to grow*.

Infinitive As Adverb

To escape, the dog leaped over the fence.

Split Infinitives and Verb Phrases

As you studied grammar in high school, you, no doubt, remember your teacher emotionally discussing the crime of splitting infinitives. Ever after, as you put pen to paper, the image of the poor, injured infinitive has haunted you.

Since the two parts of the infinitive are generally considered a single grammatical unit, they should not be split.

Example:

> **Split:** The boys wanted *to* daily *play* softball.
>
> **Revised:** The boys wanted *to play* softball daily.

Occasionally, although some grammarians may object, it is necessary to split an infinitive as there is no other place for the modifier to go and still make sense.

Example:

> The United States government expects *to* more than *double* its trade with Germany next year.

To rewrite the sentence without the split infinitive is long and cumbersome:

> The United States government expects to increase its trade with Germany by more than two hundred percent next year.

Thus, in cases like that, splitting the infinitive is acceptable .

The same rule applies to **verb phrases.** A verb phrase is composed of a helping and a main verb.

Examples:

> will be going, was running, has been seen

Since a verb phrase is considered a closely related unit, keep the phrase together. However, we often insert single word adverbs into the verb phrase without causing any awkwardness.

Examples:

> The boys were also *planning* to go.
>
> He was rapidly *running* toward the goal.

However, inserting longer word groups into the verb phrase makes awkward sentences.

Example:

> **Awkward:** George *had* by the time he was sixteen *mastered* two foreign languages.
>
> **Revised:** By the time he was sixteen, George *had mastered* two foreign languages.

Compound Subjects

So far we have been dealing with single word subjects. Now let's look at what happens when we have a compound, or more than one, subject in a sentence. Most of the time they are joined by or or and.

If two or more singular subjects are joined by *or* or *nor* they must have a singular verb. If two or more plural subjects are joined by *or* or *nor*, they must have a plural verb.

What sounds confusing is logical. Sorry, I can't say the same for all grammar rules. *Or* and *nor* indicate that only one part of the compound subject is going to act:

Example:

> Either Leah or Joel *is* going.

Together they form a singular compound subject; only one of them will be doing the action.

Either the men or the women *are going.*

Men or women takes a plural verb as both parts of the compound subject are plural, and whichever group goes, the subject still will be plural.

Now we come to an even more challenging problem. What if one subject in a compound subject is singular and the other is plural? Now what do you do? Not to worry; there is a rule for that, too.

If the subjects are joined by *or* or *nor* and one or more of them is singular and the others are plural, then the subject <u>closest</u> to the verb determines the agreement.

Example:

Neither <u>Daniel, Jack, *nor*</u> the <u>girls have read</u> the assignment.
Neither the <u>girls *nor*</u> <u>Daniel has read</u> the assignment.

Next, we will consider compound subjects joined by *and.* Although you might think compound subjects would always make the subject plural, there are exceptions. The rule reads:

When a compound subject is joined by *and,* the subject is <u>generally</u> plural and takes a plural verb.

Examples:

The <u>cat</u> and the <u>dog were taking</u> a nap.
A <u>helicopter</u> and two <u>airplanes are flying</u> over my house.
Four <u>students</u> and three <u>teachers</u> <u>are planning</u> the program.

There are two exceptions to this rule. A few compound subjects are considered as one unit, for instance: ham and eggs; corned beef and cabbage; and spaghetti and meatballs. They take a singular verb.

Example:

Ham and eggs is my favorite breakfast.

The other is when *every* or *each* is used with the subject. Either *every* or *each* in front of a compound subject requires a *singular* verb.

Every (or Each) boy and girl in the class was present. (Every boy and girl equals each one.)

Confusing Subjects

No, no! Now is not the time to throw the book down and your hands up. This is the time to hang in there.

The confusing subjects we will master in this section are those in unusual positions. No, they are not contortionists—they are just out of place in relation to their verbs. Then we will look at subjects of the linking *be* verbs, collective nouns, plural-looking nouns, indefinite pronouns, titles, and amounts or measurements.

Subject in Unusual Position

First, we'll tackle the subjects in unusual positions. No matter where the subject is found in the sentence, the subject must agree with its verb. Sometimes the verb comes before the subject, which can cause confusion.

Example:

Down the road and around the bend are two historical buildings.

Here the subject is *buildings,* not bend, so the plural subject *buildings* agrees with the plural verb, *are.* Notice the agreement is not affected by the prepositional phrases (down the road, around the bend) at the beginning of the sentence. Other inverted sentences begin with *here* or *there*.

Examples:

> There is the book I lost.
>
> Here are the tacos you ordered.

Beware of *here's* and *there's*. Both are contractions with the singular *is,* and should not be used with a plural subject.

Examples:

> **Incorrect:** Here's the books you asked me to get.
>
> **Correct:** Here's the book you asked me to get.
>
> **Plural:** Here are the books you asked me to get.

Subjects of Linking Verbs

If a sentence has a linking verb followed by a predicate nominative, it can cause an agreement problem. A predicate nominative is a word or words that rename the subject.

Jane is a doctor. *Jane* is the subject, *is* the linking verb — linking Jane with doctor. *Doctor* is a predicate nominative giving another name for Jane.

As always, the linking verb must agree with the subject in number. It does not matter whether the predicate nominative does or not.

Safer cars are one *reason* traffic fatalities are down. (*Reason* is the predicate nominative.)

One *reason* for decreased traffic fatalities is safer cars. (Now *cars* is the predicate nominate.)

Collective Nouns

Collective nouns cause agreement problems because they can be singular or plural, depending on how they are used in the sentence. Would I kid you? *Band, class, church, employees, family, faculty, students, team,* and *United States* are examples of collective nouns.

If the group is considered to be a **single unit,** then the noun is considered singular and agrees with a singular verb. If the group it names is considered as **individuals** with different feelings or points or view or act independently, then the subject is plural and agrees with a plural verb.

Singular:

> The jury is deadlocked.
>
> The church meets on Sunday mornings at 9:30.

Plural:

> The faculty are discussing the proposals.
>
> The jury have not agreed on a verdict.

While you need to be aware of these distinctions when using collective nouns, the problem usually can be avoided by a change in sentence structure: The members of the jury have not agreed on a verdict. Now there is no question as to whether the verb should be singular or plural as members obviously is plural.

Plural-looking Nouns

While a noun ending in *-s* is usually plural, some are, in fact, singular in meaning.

A noun that is plural in form but singular in meaning agrees with a singular verb. Some plural-looking nouns are names of branches of knowledge: *social studies, economics, mathematics, ethics, acoustics,* et cetera. Others, like collective nouns, name a single unit or idea and so have singular meanings: *news, spaghetti, macaroni, measles.*

Examples:

Singular:

Mathematics is easy for John.

Social studies is taught in junior high school.

Watch out for the tricky ones. For example, sometimes words like *acoustics* and *ethics* are not used as names of branches of knowledge but indicate qualities or characteristics. Then, their meanings are plural. Conversely, words like *pliers, scissors,* and *eyeglasses,* although they name single items, usually take plural verbs. If in doubt, consult your dictionary. How's that for a cop-out?

Plural:

The ethics of the city council were questioned.

Your eyeglasses are on the table.

Indefinite Pronouns

Depending on its form and meaning, an indefinite pronoun can agree with either a singular or plural verb. There are three groups of indefinite pronouns. Some are always singular, some always plural, and some that can be either. The third group, of course, is where the trouble starts.

Indefinite Pronouns

Singular: another, anybody, anyone, anything, each, either, everybody, everyone, everything, little, much, neither, nobody, no one, nothing, one, other, somebody, someone, something

Plural: both, few, many, others, several

Singular or Plural: all, any, more, most, none, some

> **Always singular:**
>> Neither of the cars is running well.
>>
>> Much of the house was damaged.
>
> **Always plural:**
>> Both of the girls are singing at the concert in January.
>>
>> Many of the people were unhappy.
>
> **Either singular or plural:**
>> All of the chili was eaten.
>>
>> All of the cars in the parking lot are red.

When dealing with the third group, the objects of the prepositional phrase following the indefinite pronoun determine whether the verb is singular or plural. This is an exception to ignoring the information in a prepositional phrase when determining if a subject is singular or plural. Since *chili* is considered one unit (it cannot be counted in individual units or parts), chili makes *all* singular. On the other hand, *cars* is plural (they can be counted as individual units or parts) and thus makes *all* plural.

Titles

Since a title of a book, song, or other work of art names one item, the title is singular and *always* takes a singular verb.

Examples:
> *Great Expectations* is a novel by Charles Dickens.
>
> *Field & Stream* is a sports magazine.

Amounts and Measurements

Many amounts and measurements express single units or ideas even though they may appear to be plural.

Singular:

> Ten dollars is all the money I have left.

> Two-thirds of the class is going.

Plural:

> Ten percent of the cars were recalled because of faulty brakes.

> Half of the cattle are ready to sell.

Pronoun and Antecedent Agreement

As you remember, a pronoun stands for, or takes the place of, a noun. An antecedent is the noun, or group of words acting as a noun, that the pronoun represents. Pronoun and antecedent must agree in number, person, and gender.

Number is either singular or plural. *Person* is divided into three groups (see the pronoun table). First person indicates the person speaking: I am going. Second is the person spoken to: Will you please close the door? Third is the person, place, thing, or idea spoken about: He was late.

Gender may be *masculine, feminine,* or *neuter.* The only pronouns that create a gender problem are third person singular. All others can apply to any of the three genders.

Third person singular masculine: he, him, his

Third person singular feminine: she, her, hers

Third person singular neuter: it, its

Examples:

Shirley received her invitation on Tuesday.

The car lost its muffler on the bumpy road.

Number Agreement of Pronouns and Antecedents

Be sure all personal pronouns and their antecedents agree in number, person, and gender. Especially check compound antecedents — those consisting of two or more nouns joined by *and*. Compound antecedents will take a plural antecedent.

Example:

As Lewis, Frank, and Henry were riding their bicycles home from the lake, they encountered a bear.

However, if two or more singular antecedents are joined by *or* or *nor*, then a singular personal pronoun is used.

Example:

Neither Frank nor Henry stopped his bike to watch the bear.

CASE OF NOUNS AND PRONOUNS

Case is the form of a noun or pronoun that indicates how it is used in a sentence.

Use the *nominative case* for the subject of a verb and for a predicate nominate. Use the *objective* case for the object of any verb, verbal, or preposition.

The Cases of Personal Pronouns

Singular:
Nominative: I; you; he, she, it
Objective: me; you; him, her, it
Possessive: my, mine; your, yours; his, her, hers, its

Plural:
Nominative: we; you; they
Objective: us; you; them
Possessive: our, ours; your, yours; their, theirs

Gender and Person Shifts

Be careful not to shift either gender or person when using personal pronouns with antecedents.

Shift in person:

Tom is working on a doctorate degree and you will have to work long hours if you want to get it finished.

Correct:

Tom is working on a doctorate degree and he will have to work long hours if he wants to get it finished.

Shift in gender:

San Diego is known for its world famous zoo as well as her many other interesting sights.

Correct:

San Diego is known for its world famous zoo as well as its many other interesting sights.

Generic Masculine Pronoun

Traditionally, when an antecedent's gender is not specified as being masculine or feminine, a masculine pronoun is used.

Example:

The *customer* is waiting for *his* change.

However, in recent years the trend has been to avoid "generic" pronouns by rephrasing the sentence.

Examples:

> The customer is waiting for *the* change.
>
> The customers are waiting for *their* change.

Adjectives and Adverbs

Adjectives and adverbs are the stuff of which great writing is made. They are the words that paint the pictures for the readers so they see what the writers see. Like all other parts of speech, rules govern their use.

Different forms of adjectives and adverbs have forms that show *degrees of comparison.*

The *positive* degree is the basic form. Definitions are listed under it in the dictionary, and it is used when no comparison is being made.

Example:

> It was a *good* dinner.

When comparing two persons, places, things, or ideas, you will use the comparative degree.

Example:

> That was a *better* dinner than last night's.

And, to compare three or more persons, places, things, or ideas, you use the *superlative* degree.

Example:

> It was the *best* dinner I have ever eaten.

Regular Forms

Most adjectives form their comparatives and superlatives in regular ways. The rules for forming the comparative and superlative depend on the number of syllables in the word. Like verbs, adjectives and adverbs have regular and irregular forms.

To form the comparative degree of <u>most</u> one- and two- syllable modifiers, use *-er* or *more*. To form the superlative degree of <u>most</u> one- and two-syllable modifiers, use *-est* or *most.*

While the majority of one and two-syllable words form their comparative and superlative words with *-er* and *-est*, sometimes it is necessary to use *more* or *most*. When *-er* or *-est* sounds awkward on the end of the word, you need to use *more* or *most*.

Examples:

    loster, lostest; famouser, famousest

These not only sound awkward, but are difficult to pronounce. Thus, they should be: more lost, most lost and more famous, most famous. These sound much better to the ear and are easier on the tongue.

If the modifier has three or more syllables it <u>always</u> uses *more* and *most*.

And, it doesn't matter how many syllables adverbs have, their comparative and superlative forms <u>always</u> are formed with *more* and *most*. Since most adverbs end with *-ly*, adding an *-er* or *-est* suffix is awkward.

When doing comparisons opposite more and most, use *less* and *least* to form the comparative and superlative of most of them.

Examples:

| able | less able | least able |
| exciting | less exciting | least exciting |

Irregular Forms

A few commonly used adjectives and adverbs form their comparative and superlative degrees in irregular and unpredictable ways. (Another one of the fun things about the English language.) There really is nothing to do but memorize them—or look them up each time you need to use them.

Irregular Modifiers

Positive	Comparative	Superlative
bad	worse	worst
badly	worse	worst
far	farther	farthest
far	further	furthest
good	better	best
ill	worse	worst
late	later	last or latest
little (amount)	less	least
many	more	most
much	more	most
well	better	best

Usage note: Do not use both an -er and more (less) or -est and most (least) with the same modifier. Things are not "more better." One comparative form is enough.

Comparisons

The basic rule of comparisons is that if you are comparing two persons, places, things, or ideas you use the comparative form (*-er, more, less*). If you are comparing three or more persons, places, things, or ideas you use the superlative (*-est, most, least*).

Examples:

> **Comparative:** I like the green jacket *better* than the blue one.
>
> **Superlative:** I like the purple jacket *best* of all.

While you normally will have little difficulty with comparatives, you unintentionally may compare two or more unrelated items. Be sure your sentence compares only items of a similar kind. If it doesn't, it is necessary to rephrase the sentence so the comparison is properly balanced. An unbalanced comparison is illogical and thus may be unintentionally humorous.

Example:

> **Unbalanced:** A chicken's *egg* is bigger than a *robin*.
>
> **Balanced:** A chicken's *egg* is bigger than a *robin's egg*.

Errors in usage also can occur when comparing one member of a group with the rest of the same group. In such comparisons, it is essential to include either the word *other* or the word *else* in the comparison. Unless *other* or *else* is included, an illogical comparison is created.

Examples:

> **Illogical:** Jane is taller than any member of her class.
>
> **Logical:** Jane is taller than any *other* member of her class.
>
> **Illogical:** Sam ran faster than anyone in the race.
>
> **Logical:** Sam ran faster than anyone *else* in the race.

Jane cannot be taller than herself, so *other* is needed to make the statement logical. Since Sam obviously cannot run faster than himself, *else* is necessary to clarify the meaning.

Basic Sentence Parts

In order to be grammatically correct, a sentence must have two parts: a *complete subject* and a *complete predicate*. Together, they express a complete thought.

The complete subject includes a noun or pronoun and names the person, place, thing, or idea that the sentence is about. The complete predicate includes a verb or verb phrase that tells something about the subject. The complete subject (cs) and complete predicate (cp) each may consist of one or more words:

Examples:

We | are leaving for California tomorrow.

cs | complete predicate - - - - - - - - - - - -

The young boys, fearing they would be identified, | ran.

complete subject - - - - - - - - - - - - - - - - - - - - - - - -| cp

Joe | talked.

cs | cp

A sentence must have a complete subject and a complete predicate, if either or both are missing the result is a sentence fragment. A *fragment* does not express a complete thought.

Examples of fragments:

going to the store (no subject)

The girls, laughing and talking, (no verb)

over the hill and far away (no subject or verb)

While we often speak in fragments, our voice, gestures, tone, and facial expressions help listeners understand what we mean. However, fragments do not work in written communication. But it is   permissible to use fragments in dialogue, because good dialogue imitates speech. Another use is in an *elliptical sentence* in which the missing word or words are obvious and can be easily understood. These should, however, be used sparingly.

Examples:
> **Elliptical sentences:**
>> (I) thank you.
>>
>> John is taller than she (is tall).

Compound Subject and Verb

A compound subject consists of two or more subjects that have the same verb. They are joined by a conjunction such as *and* or *or*.

Example:
> Hard work, long hours, perseverance, and enthusiasm are necessary ingredients for success.

Like subjects, verbs can be compound. To be compound, two or more verbs must have the same subject and be joined by a conjunction such as *and* or *or*.

Examples:
> The children ran and played for hours.
>
> John ran to the bank, jumped into the river, and swam across to the other side.

Some sentences contain both a compound subject and a compound verb.

Example:
> The teacher and students read and discussed *Julius Caesar* by William Shakespeare.

"Hidden" Subjects

While subjects are usually where they are easily found, some are not. For instance, in sentences that give orders or directions, you is understood to be the subject.

Example:

(You) Please go to the store and buy some bread.

Before the cake burns, (you) take it out of the oven.

Sometimes the usual subject/verb order is reversed or inverted. Included are sentences starting with *there* or *here* and most sentences that ask a question. However, questions that begin with an interrogatory adjective or pronoun: *what, which, whose, who, when, why, where,* or *how* may be in the regular subject/verb order. In addition, sentences may be inverted for greater emphasis.

Examples of questions in inverted subject/verb order:

Are you planning to go with me?

Where is the building located?

Examples of questions in regular subject/verb order:

Who ran through the yard?

Which actor won the award?

Here and *there* often are found at the beginning of inverted sentences. However they are never the subject—unless they are referred to as a word.

Examples:

As subject:

Here often is found at the beginning of an inverted sentence.

Not a subject:

> Here <u>are</u> the <u>reports</u> you wanted.
>
> There <u>is</u> my lost <u>dog.</u>

Sentences may have subjects and verbs in inverted order so that the subject can receive greater emphasis. As you read a sentence you tend to wind down and forget important words if they occur early in the sentence.

Notice how the emphasis is lost when the following sentences are phrased in the regular subject/verb order.

> The ravenous <u>dogs</u> prowled in the dark alley behind the deserted building.
>
> The <u>leopard hovered</u> high up in the tree.

However, inverting the sentence order puts the emphasis on *dogs* and *leopards*.

Examples:

> In the dark alley behind the deserted building <u>prowled</u> the ravenous <u>dogs.</u>
>
> High up in the tree <u>hovered</u> the <u>leopard.</u>

Hint: Mentally rearranging an inverted sentence can help you locate the subject.

Conclusion

Now that you have completed your grammar review, you are on your way to sending editors error-free manuscripts.

Chapter 15:

Style Review

As you write and rewrite, you need to consider what voice to use, what words to capitalize, where to place punctuation, et cetera. This chapter will help you solve these problems.

Active and Passive Voice

The *voice* of the verb is active or passive, depending on whether the subject is doing or receiving the action.

When the subject performs the action, the verb is *active.*

When its action is performed upon the subject, the verb is *passive.*

Examples:

> **Active:** The pitcher *threw the ball.*
>
> **Passive:** The ball *was thrown* by the pitcher.

A *passive verb* consists of a verb phrase made from a form of *be* and the *past participle* of a transitive verb.

Use the active voice whenever possible.

Use the passive voice to emphasize the receiver of an action rather than the performer of the action.

Example:

> The bomb *was planted* by an unidentified terrorist.

Also, use the passive voice to point out the receiver of an action when the performer is unknown or unimportant and is not named in the sentence.

Example:

> The toll booth *was closed* at 7 p.m.

Capitalization

Capital letters serve as clues that the word or words are something special. As writers, we must use them properly.

Capitalize the first word in a sentence. Also capitalize the first word of a quotation that is a complete sentence.

Examples:

> Henry asked, "Are you going with us?"
>
> "Yes, we are going with you," answered Lori.

A "he said/she said" phrase in the middle of quoted material that is one *continuous sentence* is <u>not</u> capitalized. Only the first word of the quotation gets a capital letter.

Example:

> "On your way to the store," said mother, "please stop at the cleaners and pick up my dress."

However, if the "he said/she said" is between *two complete* sentences, both sentences start with capital letters.

Example:

> "We are going to the zoo," Robin shouted. "I love watching the monkeys."

If the quotation is not a complete sentence and is contained within a longer sentence, the first word of the quotation is not capitalized.

Example:

> Sometimes in severe weather we wonder whatever happened to the post office motto, "neither snow nor rain nor heat" would stop the mail from getting through.

After a Colon

If the first word after a colon begins a complete sentence that first word is capitalized. However, if that first word is the first word in a list, it is not capitalized. **Caution:** Be very sure whatever follows the colon is a complete sentence before capitalizing the first word.

Examples:

> Incorrect: They could not believe what they read: No Parking.
>
> Correct: They could not believe what they read: The sign said "No Parking."

List: She opened her presents: two necklaces, three blouses, and one skirt.

The first word in interjections and question fragments should be capitalized. This rule also includes exclamatory interjections.

Examples:

What? For me? Why not? Ouch! Super! Wow!

Poetry

In *most* cases the first word in each *line* of poetry is capitalized.

I and O

Words like *I* and *O* are <u>always</u> capitalized no matter where they appear in the sentence.

Note: Don't confuse *O* and *oh*. The word oh is only capitalized when it is the first word in a sentence.

Proper Nouns

Since proper nouns name a specific person, place, thing, or idea, they are <u>always</u> capitalized. If there is more than one part, capitalize the beginning letter of each part.

Examples:

Jerome Noel, Leah M. Kennedy, D. E. Davies

Note: When a surname consists of more than one part, check capitalization carefully. Some, e.g., McDonald and St. Thomas, capitalize both parts. Others beginning with *de, D' la, le, Mac, van,* or *von,* are not consistent and sometimes are capitalized and other times are not. If in doubt, check it out.

Capitalize the proper names of animals.

Examples:

Lassie, the dog; Kermit, the frog.

Geographical and Place Names

Names of <u>specific</u> geographical locations should be capitalized:

Geographical Name Examples:

Streets: 25th Street; Topeka Boulevard

Towns & Cities: Leroy, Los Angeles, Wichita

Counties: Pottawatomie County, Lake County

States & Provinces: Kansas, Indiana, Ontario

Nations: United States of America, England, France

Continents: Arctic, South America

Mountains: the Rocky Mountains

Valleys & Deserts: Death Valley, Sahara Desert

Islands: the Virgin Islands

Sections of a Country: the Midwest, the East

Scenic Spots: Mammoth Cave, Lookout Mountain

Rivers & Falls: Mississippi River, Niagara Falls

Lakes & Bays: Lake Michigan, Massachusetts Bay

Oceans & Seas: Pacific Ocean, the Mediterranean Sea

Celestial Bodies: Mars, the Little Dipper

Note: The earth, moon, and sun do <u>not</u> follow this rule. The moon and sun are not capitalized. However, *earth* may be, depending on how it is used in the sentence. If the word *earth* is preceded by the article *the,* it is not capitalized. However, when using *Earth* as one of the planets, it is capitalized.

Examples:

Not Capitalized: Icarus should have flown nearer the earth instead of heading toward the sun.

Capitalized: The boys hope one day to leave Earth and travel to Mars.

Compass Points

Some confusion exists as to whether compass points should be capitalized. If the word *north,* for example, indicates a direction, it is not capitalized. However, if North designates a specific, location it is capitalized.

Examples:

The pioneers headed *west* from St. Joseph, Missouri.

We are visiting some friends in the *Southeast.*

Monuments, Buildings & Meeting Rooms

The place names of monuments, buildings, and meeting rooms must be capitalized.

Examples: Specific Places

Monuments & Memorials: the Washington Monument; the Viet Nam Memorial

Buildings: the Pentagon; the Coliseum

School & Meeting Rooms: Room 210; the Blue Room; the Oval Office

However, you do not capitalize theater, hotel, high school, or university unless it is part of a proper name.

Examples:

Not capitalized: My brother is a freshman in high school.

Capitalized: My brother attends Frankfort High School.

In addition, the word *room* is only capitalized when it refers to a specific room and is connected with a name, letter, or number.

Examples:

Not capitalized: They are redecorating the dining room.

Capitalized: The class meeting is in Room 121.

OTHER PROPER NOUNS

There are specific capitalization customs regarding references to time and history. Capitalize the names of specific events and periods of time.

Specific Events & Times

Historic Periods: the Dark Ages

Historic Events: the Civil War

Documents & Laws: the Declaration of Independence; the Voting Rights Act

Days: Sunday

Months: January

Holidays: Memorial Day

Religious Days: Easter, Yom Kippur

Special Events: the World Series, the Boston Marathon

Do not capitalize the seasons unless they are part of a proper noun.

Example:

Winter Carnival

The names of various organizations, government bodies, political parties, races, and nationalities, as well as the languages spoken by different groups are capitalized.

Specific Groups and Languages

Clubs: Elks Club, Lions Club, Topeka Writers' Club

Organizations: United Mine Workers, American Heart Association

Institutions: Indiana University, St. Francis Hospital

Businesses: General Motors, 3-M Corporation

Government Bodies: the House of Representatives, Commerce Department

Political Parties: the Republicans, the Socialist Party

Races: Caucasian, Negro, Mongoloid

Nationalities: German, Spanish, American

Languages: English, Japanese, Russian

Note: Do not capitalize words like black or white when referring to race.

Religions, Deities, & Religious Scriptures

All of the world's religions have words that refer to their important and sacred beliefs. Even if you are not a believer in a particular faith, it is courteous and necessary to capitalize references to each religion.

However, when writing about mythological gods and goddesses, capitalization of religious references is not required. Although the words *god* and *goddess* are <u>not</u> capitalized, their proper names are:

Examples:

the god Jupiter; the goddess Venus

More Rules

Names of awards should be capitalized.

Example:

> the Golden Quill Award

The names of *specific* types of air, sea, land, and space craft are capitalized. However, do <u>not</u> capitalize the word the preceding a name unless it is part of the official name:

> **Air:** Boeing 737
> **Land:** the Model A
> **Sea:** Titanic
> **Space:** Challenger

Brand names, whether used as adjectives or as full trademark names, are capitalized. If the full trademark name is used, all the words in the name are considered a proper noun. They are capitalized.

When a brand name is used as a proper adjective followed by a common noun, the brand name is capitalized, but the common noun is not.

Examples: a Ford truck

> a Ford Bronco

A proper adjective is formed from a proper noun or is a proper noun used as an adjective. You should capitalize <u>most</u> proper adjectives. Some, however, like *french fries* and *teddy bear* have been used together so long that they no longer are capitalized.

When a prefix precedes a proper adjective, the prefix is not capitalized unless it refers to a nationality. In any hyphenated adjective, only capitalize the proper adjective.

Examples:

> pre-Inca culture; pro-American reaction; Afro-American; French-speaking Canadians.

TITLES OF PEOPLE AND WORKS

Capitalize titles of people and of works.

Of People

A person's title is capitalized when it is followed by the person's name or used in direct address.

Examples:

> Prof., Dr., Sir
>
> Lord Fisher
>
> Sir Laurence Olivier
>
> **Direct address:** Is there anything else, Sir?
>
> **In general reference:** The doctor returned the call.

However, a title is <u>always</u> capitalized if it is for an exceptionally high ranking official (President, Vice-President, Chief Justice, Queen of England).

Examples:

> The President and Vice-President will fly by helicopter to the meeting.
>
> The Chief Justice and the eight justices of the Supreme Court will hear the case on Wednesday.

If a title is compound, capitalize all important words but <u>not</u> the prefixes or suffixes added to them.

Examples:

> ex-Senator Smith, Governor-elect Monroe

When referring to family members, capitalize a title showing family relationship when the title is used with the person's name or in direct address. If the title refers to a specific person, the title may be capitalized *except* when it comes after a possessive noun or pronoun. If the name is used as a common noun, then the capital letter is dropped.

Examples with capitals:

When is Aunt Marilyn coming to visit?

I'll be home at 9 p.m., Mom.

Examples without capitals:

Mr. Jones became a grandfather Thursday.

I wonder where my mom put my lunch.

Abbreviations of titles before and after names are capitalized. The most common ones are Mr., Mrs., Jr., and Sr.

Examples:

Mrs. Amy Jackson, Mr. James Stuart, Sr.

Note: Although Ms. ends with a period it is <u>not</u> an abbreviation. It can be used before a proper name to refer to either a single or a married woman.

Of Works

The first word and all other important words in the titles of books, periodicals, poems, stories, plays, paintings, and other works of art are capitalized. The words *a, an,* and *the* are <u>only</u> capitalized when they are the first word of the title. <u>Only</u> capitalize conjunctions and prepositions of less than five letters if they are the first word in the title. Since adjectives, nouns, pronouns, verbs, and adverbs are considered important words they are <u>always</u> capitalized. The same rules apply to subtitles.

Title examples:

> **Book:** *A Tale of Two Cities*
> **Periodical:** *Journal of Graphoanalysis*
> **Poem:** "The House with Nobody in It"
> **Story:** "The Contest of the Archers"
> **Play:** *The Taming of the Shrew*
> **Painting:** *Weaver's Cycle:* March of the Weavers
> **Music:** "There's a Tree in the Meadow"

Of Courses

If a course title refers to a language or is followed by a number, it is capitalized.

Examples:

> **With capitals:** English; Spanish III; American History 101
> **Without capitals:** science; history; auto mechanics

In Letter Writing

Finally, the first word and all nouns in letter salutations and the first word in letter closings are capitalized.

Examples:

> **Salutations:** Dear Sir; Gentlemen; My darling Penny
> **Closing:** Very truly yours; Sincerely; With deepest sympathy

ABBREVIATION RULES

Abbreviations were created to save time and space. Some have become so common and popular, such as auto, memo, exam, that we often no longer think of them as abbreviations. There are rules governing their use.

Titles of People

Unless a person uses initials as part of his or her given name, use the full given name in formal writing. However, in addresses or lists the use of initials is acceptable.

> **Formal:** My cousin Martin Dedrick (not M. Dedrick) is coming for a visit.

> **In address or list:** Martin Dedrick or M. Dedrick

An abbreviation of social titles before a proper name begins with a capital letter and ends with a period. Unlike abbreviations of names, it is acceptable to use them in formal writing. However, do not use an abbreviated title unless a proper name follows it.

Examples:

> **Incorrect:** The Mr. is out of town.

> **Correct:** Mr. Frink is out of town.

Abbreviations of other titles used before a proper name begin with a capital letter and end with a period. If only the surname is given, write out the title. However, they are not often used in formal writing.

Example:

> **Incorrect:** Gen. Patton conducted the meeting.

> **Correct:** General Patton conducted the meeting.

> Gen. George Patton conducted the meeting.

The exception to this is *Dr.* which is abbreviated before a proper noun just like *Mr.* and *Mrs.* are.

Certain religious titles (Reverend, Father, Sister, Brother) and the title *Honorable* are customarily <u>not</u> abbreviated even when a first name or initials are used with them.

Abbreviations of titles <u>after</u> a name begin with a capital letter and end with a period. They can be used in any type of writing. However, do not abbreviate *Junior, Senior,* or academic degrees, unless they follow a proper name.

Time Reference

Abbreviations for clocked time (sec.; min.; hr.) begin with a small letter and end with a period. Abbreviations for days of the week (Sun., Mon.) and months of the year (Jan., Feb.) begin with a capital letter and end with a period. Abbreviations are not used in formal writing.

Examples:

> **Incorrect:** We will meet the first Tues. in Aug.
>
> **Correct:** We will meet the first Tuesday in August.

Abbreviations of time before noon and after noon can be either capital letters followed by periods or small letters followed by periods. Both are acceptable and can be used in any type of writing. However, they only are used when referring to an exact time of day using numerals, otherwise write the words out.

Examples:

> **Incorrect:** We will be leaving in the a.m.
>
> **Correct:** We will be leaving before noon.
>
> We will be leaving at 10:00 a.m.

Abbreviations for historic dates before and after the birth of Christ are capital letters followed by periods: *B.C.* and *A.D.* They can be used in any type of writing.

Note: B.C. is placed <u>after</u> the number it refers to. A.D. can be before or after the number <u>unless</u> the word century is spelled out. If century is spelled out, then A.D. goes after it.

Examples:

The event occurred about 1000 A.D.

The event occurred about A.D. 1000.

The sixth century A.D. was an interesting time.

Geographic Locations

Abbreviations of names of geographic locations can be confusing. These abbreviations generally are used only in addresses, lists, charts, and informal writing. Abbreviations for geographic terms before or after a proper noun begin with a capital letter and end with a period.

Examples:

Ave.; Dist.; Dr.; Natl.

Two sets of abbreviations exist for states: the traditional set and the newer two-letter official post office abbreviation. Traditional state abbreviations begin with a capital letter and end with a period. On the other hand, the postal abbreviation consists of two capital letters and no period. Neither is used often in formal writing.

Note: The traditional abbreviation for the District of Columbia is D.C. It is the one to use in formal writing after the word Washington.

One exception to the use of abbreviations in formal writing is when referring to the U.S.S.R. or the U.S. These abbreviations are acceptable in formal writing.

Measurements and Numbers

Use small letters and periods to abbreviate traditional measurements. However, metric measurement abbreviations are formed with small letters and no period. Do not use these abbreviations in formal writing, except with numerals. A dictionary or almanac will give you a complete listing of all measurements and their abbreviations.

Numbers or amounts of less than one hundred and any other numbers that can be written in two words or less should be spelled out in formal writing.

Examples:

There are five boys going to the show.

They raised six thousand dollars for charity.

A crowd of 752 watched the parade.

When a number occurs at the beginning of a sentence, it must be spelled out. To avoid spelling out large numbers, try to place the numbers elsewhere in the sentence.

Examples:

Four hundred and twenty-nine pounds of food were collected to help feed the needy.

To help feed the needy, they collected 429 pounds of food.

Numerals are used to refer to fractions, decimals, and percentages. Be sure **not** to start a sentence with them.

Examples:

Susie is 33 ½ inches tall.

He received 66 percent of the vote.

The answer to that question is 29.7.

In Dates

Numerals are used when writing dates.

Example:

The test was scheduled for April 2, 1989.

In Addresses

Numerals are used when writing addresses.

Example:

135 West 5th Street.

Sometimes you find words or numbers you're not sure if it is proper to abbreviate. Then the best advice is: "If in doubt, spell it out."

Other Names

A variety of methods exist for abbreviating names of businesses, organizations,

government agencies and other groups. However, some of them are not considered appropriate for formal writing.

In Business Names

When a word is abbreviated in a business name it begins with a capital letter and ends with a period.

Examples:

Bros.; Co.; Mfg.

In formal writing, limit the use of abbreviations to *Inc.* and *Ltd.*

Initial Abbreviations

Sometimes names are shortened so that only the first letter of each word in the name is used. The word is pronounced letter by letter and is called an initial abbreviation. These abbreviations use all capital letters and no periods and are often used in formal writing.

Examples:

> NRA (National Rifle Association); NBC (National Broadcasting Company); FBI (Federal Bureau of Investigation)

Acronyms

When the initials blend together and are pronounced as a single word, they are called acronyms.

Examples:

> WAC (Women's Army Corps); LISA (Low Input Sustainable Agriculture); BART (Bay Area Rapid Transit)

PUNCTUATION

Now we come to a section that often causes problems. Where do all those punctuation marks go? Putting them in the wrong places may just indicate that we don't understand the rules. We need to use punctuation carefully because a misplaced comma can alter the meaning. Attorneys are very conscious of punctuation, and I once heard of a criminal case being dismissed because a comma was in the wrong place and had altered the meaning.

Probably none of our punctuation errors will have that serious a consequence. However, we should use punctuation marks correctly so there will be no chance for our readers to misunderstand what we have to say.

End Marks

Three common end marks are used in writing: the period (.), the question mark (?), and the exclamation mark (!). Each brings readers to a stop and lets them know you have completed a thought. Use end marks to end all sentences and some phrases. Choosing end marks carefully can convey the desired emotion or tone of the sentence.

Examples:

We are going. We are going? We are going!

Periods

Use a period if the statement is a declarative sentence, a mild imperative, or an indirect question. An indirect question does not require an answer.

Examples:

Declarative: We bought a book.

Mild imperative: Close the window.

Indirect question: I asked him what time we were leaving.

Question Marks

A question mark ends a direct question, an incomplete question, or a statement intended as a question. A direct question requires an answer and must end with a question mark. Sometimes, only a part of the question is asked and the rest is understood. Or a question may be phrased as a declarative sentence, and the only clue a reader will have that it is a question is the question mark at the end.

Examples:

Direct question: Do you like the red or pink dress better?

Incomplete question: When? Which one?

Statement as question: Cheryl is coming too?

In addition to ending interrogative sentences, a question mark in parentheses (?) after a detail or statistic indicates the writer is not sure it is correct. This alerts readers not to accept the information as fact without checking it out. Use of the question mark in this way, however, should be limited to things you cannot verify. The question mark should not be used to avoid doing research.

Example:

Julius Caesar was born in 102 B.C. (?)

Do <u>not</u> use the question mark in parenthesis to indicate humor or irony. Choose your words carefully, and they will provide the tone you wish to convey.

Examples:

Incorrect: The skillful (?) carpenter left a two inch gap in the wall.

Correct: The presumably skillful carpenter left a two-inch gap in the wall.

Exclamation Marks

To make a sentence show strong emotion use an exclamation mark. It ends an exclamatory sentence, a forceful imperative sentence, or an interjection expressing strong emotion.

Examples:

Exclamatory: He spent $50 for that dinner!

Strong imperative: Do it now!

Strong interjection: Fantastic! Super!

On occasion you may use a strong interjection before a short exclamatory sentence. You can choose to use either a comma or an exclamation mark after the interjection.

Examples:

With comma: Oh dear, we are late!

With exclamation mark: Oh dear! We are late!

A word of caution: Too many exclamation marks will bore your readers. Nothing is *that* exciting. Also, avoid the temptation to put two or three at the end of a single sentence, which does nothing except label you as an amateur writer. A limit of one end mark per sentence, please.

Note: If you end a sentence with an abbreviation that requires a period, do not add an extra period as an end mark. If the abbreviation is elsewhere in the sentence and some other form of punctuation needs to follow it, be sure to use it.

Examples:

> **Incorrect:** The meeting will start promptly at 10:30 a.m..
>
> **Correct:** The meeting will start promptly at 10:30 a.m.
>
> > Although the meeting will start promptly at 10:30 a.m., I will be late.

Commas

Since we use commas more than any other punctuation mark, they also cause the most problems. Commas indicate that readers should take a short pause, but not as long as for a period. They also may separate items, phrases, or clauses.

In Compound Sentences

A comma can separate independent clauses in a compound sentence. A compound sentence consists of two or more independent clauses, which could stand as sentences by themselves. These clauses are joined by one of the coordinating conjunctions: *and, or, nor, for, but, yet,* or *so.* Be sure, however, that you have written two complete sentences joined by a coordinating conjunction before you insert a comma.

Examples:

> **Incorrect:** He went to the park, and then went swimming.
>
> **Correct:** He went to the park, and then he went swimming.

Note: If two complete sentences are very short, the comma can be left out.

> **Example:** He liked to hunt but she liked to sew.

In Series

A series of words, phrases, or clauses in a sentence are separated by commas.

Examples:

> **Words:** He bought toothpaste, deodorant, and razor blades.
>
> **Prepositional Phrases:** We searched for the hammer in the house, in the garage, and in the yard.
>
> **Clauses:** The classroom was full of students who read their assignments, who wrote their papers, and who turned in their projects.

Note: It is acceptable to omit the comma before the and as long as you follow a consistent usage pattern. However, since there are times it is needed to prevent confusion, use of the comma is recommended.

Examples:

> **Correct:** He ran, skipped and jumped.
>
> **Confusing:** The noisy crowd, the barking dogs and children created quite an uproar.
>
> **Clear:** The noisy crowd, the barking dogs, and children created quite an uproar.

Note: You do not need commas in a series if all the items are separated by conjunctions.

Example:

> The boys ran *and* played *and* wrestled all afternoon.

In addition, pairs of items used together so frequently that they are thought of as one item do not need commas between them.

Example:

> He ordered spaghetti and meatballs, bread and butter, and coffee and cream.

Adjectives

Adjectives of equal rank (coordinate adjectives) should be separated by commas. Adjectives are coordinate if:

(1) You can put an *and* between them, and the meaning of the sentence stays the same;

(2) You can switch their position, and the sentence still sounds grammatically correct.

If both are true, then the adjectives are of equal rank and you need a comma between them.

Example:

> The cat's sleek, shiny coat glistened in the sun.

However, if the adjectives must remain in a particular order, do not separate them with a comma. These are called *cumulative adjectives*. They must be in a specific order for the sentence to retain its intended meaning.

Example:

> A few well-dressed men were having a meeting.

After Introductory Material

Introductory material may consist of words, phrases, or clauses. You need a comma after it.

Examples:

Words:

Yes, I will meet you at 6:30 p.m.

Matt, will you answer the door.

Hurriedly, he ran to catch the bus.

Phrases:

In a dark corner of the basement, I found the missing kitten.

Leaping high in the air, the fielder caught the ball.

Clauses:

When the cake was done, she took it out of the oven.

With Parenthetical Expressions

A parenthetical expression is a word or phrase not related to the rest of the sentence, and it interrupts the general flow of the sentence. These parenthetical expressions include nouns of direct address, i.e. Mother, Steve, Mrs. Smith; some adverbs such as *however, furthermore, nevertheless;* contrasting expressions such as *not here, not his, not this one;* and common expressions such as *in my opinion, on the other hand, of course.* Set parenthetical expressions off from the rest of the sentence with commas. If the expression occurs within the sentence, use commas on both sides of the expression. If the expression occurs at the beginning or end of a sentence, only one comma is needed.

Examples:

In middle:

Wait here, Jane, until we return.

Dale, in my opinion, needs to see a doctor.

At beginning:

Jane, wait here until we return.

In my opinion, Dale needs to see a doctor.

At end:

> Wait here until we return, Jane.
>
> Dale needs to see a doctor, in my opinion.

Essential and Nonessential Expressions

It is important to learn to distinguish between essential and nonessential expressions, sometimes called restrictive and nonrestrictive. Use commas to set off nonessential expressions.

Essential Expressions

An essential expression provides needed information for the reader. It cannot be removed without changing the meaning of the sentence. In the following sentence the clause following *girl* is needed to identify *which* girl:

> The girl who is wearing a red dress is my niece.

Nonessential Expressions

In the following example the clause is not essential to the girl's identity as we know her name.

Example:

> Lisa Porter, who is wearing a red dress, is my niece.

OTHER USES

Dates

If dates contain numbers they need commas. A date consisting of two or more parts needs a comma after each item <u>except</u> when the month is followed by the day.

Examples:

> On Friday, April 20, I will be flying to Los Angeles.

> After much discussion, June 10, 1991, was decided upon for the grand opening.

Note: The comma is optional if the date only consists of the month and the year.

Examples:

> The president reported that sales for May, 1985, were up.
>
> The president reported that sales for May 1985 were up.
>
> The comma is needed if parts of a date have been joined by a preposition.

Example:

> On June 10 in 1986, we will move to our new location.

Locations

A geographical name consisting of two or more parts needs a comma after each item.

Example:

> They traveled by car from Indianapolis, Indiana, to Springfield, Illinois.

Titles

A name followed by one or more titles needs a comma after the name and after each title.

Example:

> Did you know that Henry J. Stevenson, Jr., is now working for Gavit, Richardson, and Draper, Incorporated?

Addresses

In addresses consisting of two or more parts, use a comma after each item in the address.

Example:

> His new address is John Davidson, 426 White Oak Lane, Valparaiso, Indiana 46383.

However, on an envelope, most of the commas would be omitted. In both examples, an extra space instead of a comma is left between the state and the ZIP code.

Example:

> John Davidson
>
> 426 White Oak Lane
>
> Valparaiso, Indiana 46383

Salutations and Closings

A comma is used after the salutation in a personal letter and after the closing in all letters.

> **Salutations:** Dear Mom, Dear George,
>
> **Closings:** Very truly yours, Sincerely, Cordially,

With Numbers

If a number has more than three digits, insert a comma after every third digit counting from the right.

Examples:

> 1,286   1,632,874

Exceptions:

> ZIP codes, telephone numbers, page, and serial numbers do not contain commas.

With Omissions

In an elliptical sentence, one where a word or phrase has been purposely left out, use a comma to indicate the location of the omission.

Example:

The stew cooked rapidly; the roast, slowly.

With Quotations

Set off the quoted words in a "he said/she said" quotation with a comma.

Note: See the section on use of quotation marks for more uses of the comma with direct quotations.

For Clarity

Occasionally the exact meaning of a sentence will be unclear without a comma. To avoid the chance of being misunderstood, include a comma where needed.

Examples:

Unclear: Joshua studied German and Spanish literature.

Clear: Joshua studied German, and Spanish literature.

Semicolons

The semicolon (;) alerts readers that they should pause longer than for a comma, but not as long as for a period. The semicolon can join independent sentences or clarify a possibly confusing sentence structure. It can join independent clauses not already joined by the conjunction *and, or, nor, for, but, so,* or *yet.* Remember, if the independent clauses are joined by one of those conjunctions, put a comma, not a semicolon, before the conjunction.

Since the semicolon is a stronger punctuation mark than the comma, it replaces both the comma and the conjunction. Unless the first word following the semicolon is a proper noun or a proper adjective it should not be capitalized.

Examples:

> Sam is a good tennis player, and he will represent our school in the tournament on Saturday.

> Sam is a good tennis player; he will represent our school in the tournament on Saturday.

Do <u>not,</u> however, use the semicolon to join unrelated sentences. It only should be used when there is a close relationship between them.

Examples:

> **Incorrect:** The dog was chasing a ball; school was dismissed early because of snow.

> **Correct:** Jane studied her algebra for six hours; she hoped to get an A on the final examination.

If items in a series contain commas, they should be separated by semicolons to avoid confusion. If only commas are used, readers must try to decide where one series ends and the next one begins. Use a semicolon when the items contain nonessential appositives, participial phrases, or adjective clauses.

Examples:

> **Appositive:** He was congratulated by Mr. Demarree, the football coach; Mr. Simmons, the athletic director; and Mr. Barack, the principal.

> **Participial phrases:** The dog, nipping at his heels; the cat, clawing his arm; and the bird, pecking his face, discouraged the burglar.

> **Adjective clause:** The trip, which had been planned for months; the flight, which was extremely smooth; and the scenery, which was breathtaking, contributed to a memorable vacation.

Colon

A colon's main purpose is to introduce various items. One of the most important things it introduces is a list. It is used after an independent clause and before a list of items.

Examples:

> A well-stocked medicine cabinet contains the following items: gauze pads, adhesive tape, bandages, and cotton balls.
>
> I bought several camera accessories on sale: a fancy strap, a tripod, and a telephoto lens.

Certain quotations are introduced by a colon. If a quotation is formal or lengthy or does not contain a "he said/she said" phrase, use a colon to introduce it. Usually a formal quotation that requires a colon consists of more than one sentence. The best guideline is how formal a quotation it is. The more formal the quotation the more likely it is to need a colon introduction.

Do <u>not</u> use a colon to introduce a casual quoted remark or dialogue, even of more than one sentence, <u>unless</u> there is no "he said/she said" phrase.

Examples:

> **Formal:** The Queen rose from her throne and turned: "You are dismissed. I will call for you again on Tuesday."
>
> **Casual:**
>
> **Incorrect:** Brenda turned to Nathan and said: "The show starts at 6 p.m. If you don't hurry, you will be late."
>
> **Correct:** Brenda turned to Nathan and said, "The show starts at 6 p.m. If you don't hurry, you will be late."

A colon is used to introduce a sentence that either summarizes or explains the sentence before it.

Note: If a complete sentence follows the colon you need to capitalize the first word after the colon.

Example:

> My English teacher gave me some good advice: She said to study hard and turn all my assignments in on time.

A colon is used to direct attention to a formal appositive following an independent clause. Before using a colon with an appositive, be sure that the first clause is independent. If it cannot stand alone the colon will create a sentence fragment.

Examples:

> **Incorrect:** They planned: to visit a museum.
>
> **Correct:** They planned to visit a museum: Field's Museum of Natural History.

Since the colon provides a slightly more formal and commanding effect than the comma, you will have to decide which punctuation mark is appropriate for your intended tone.

Special Uses

Several special circumstances require a colon. They include: time, volume and page numbers, Biblical chapter and verse references, book subtitles, business letter salutations, and labels that introduce important information.

Examples

> **Numerals Giving the Time:** 4:52 P.M. 8:30 A.M.
>
> **Reference to Periodicals (Volume number: Page number):** *Science News* 136:268
>
> **Biblical Reference** (Chapter Number: Verse Number): John 3:16
>
> **Subtitles for Books and Magazines:** *The SHARK: Splendid Savage of the Sea*

Salutations in Business Letters: Dear Mr. White: Gentlemen: Dear Madam:

Labels Used to Signal Important Ideas: Warning: Keep this product out of the reach of children.

QUOTATION MARKS
With Direct Quotations

Since, as writers, we often use direct quotations, we need to punctuate them properly. Keep in mind that a direct quotation represents a person's exact speech or thoughts. An indirect quotation which paraphrases the person's speech or thoughts. When using a <u>direct</u> quotation, enclose it in quotation marks.

Examples:

Direct: John said, "Give me back my book."

Indirect: John told Susan she should give him back his book.

The indirect quotation lacks the strength of emphasis of the direct one. You will want to use direct quotations for emphasis whenever possible.

There are various ways to show a direct quotation. You can place the entire quotation in an uninterrupted sentence or include an introductory, concluding, or interrupting phrase with the quotation. Or you can place a quoted phrase within an otherwise complete sentence.

Reminders: Use double quotation marks to enclose a sentence that is an uninterrupted direct quote. Be sure to begin each complete sentence of quotation with a capital letter.

Examples:

Uninterrupted: "It is impossible to love and be wise."—Francis Bacon

Introductory Expression: Francis Bacon wrote, "It is impossible to love and be wise."

Concluding Expression: "It is impossible to love and be wise," wrote Francis Bacon.

Interrupting Expression: "It is impossible," wrote Francis Bacon, "to love and be wise."

When a direct quotation follows an introductory expression, put a comma or a colon after the introductory expression. Then, write the quotation as a full sentence. You may use a "he said/she said" expression to indicate who is speaking. However, if you do not use a "he said/she said" expression to introduce it, or if the introductory phrase carries a more formal tone, use a colon instead of a comma.

Examples:

The President turned to the reporters: "We have just completed a new trade agreement with Germany."

Soberly the doctor stated: "Your father is in critical condition."

While a comma appears to be correct in the second example, the formal tone of the statement makes the colon a better choice.

When the "he said/she said" or some other concluding expression follows a direct quotation, write the quotation as a full sentence ending with a comma, question mark, or exclamation mark inside the quotation mark. Then add your concluding expression.

Examples:

"We will meet you at the park," said Joshua.

"Will you meet us at the park?" asked Joshua.

"The car is gone!" cried Susie.

At times you will want to interrupt a direct quote with a "he said/she said" expression. One situation is when using a quotation lengthy enough to be a paragraph, or almost a paragraph, by itself. It is a good idea to start and/or end the paragraph with interesting quoted material and give the person's name and qualifications, if necessary, in the middle of it.

When interrupting a direct quotation that is one sentence long, end the first part of it with a comma and a quotation mark. Then, place a comma after the interrupting expression and continue with a new quotation mark and the rest of the quotation. End the quoted sentence with a singular quotation mark.

Example:

> "When I told her I was leaving," said Nathan, "Mom told me to be home by 10 p.m."

When interrupting a direct quotation of two sentences, end the first quoted sentence with a comma, question mark, or exclamation mark, and a quotation mark. Place a period after the interrupter and write the second sentence as a full quotation.

Example:

> "There are indeed specific human virtues, but they are those necessary to existence, like patience and courage," said George Santayana in *Reason in Religion*. "Supported on these indispensable habits, mankind always carries an indefinite load of misery and vice."

With Other Punctuation Marks

A comma or a period is always placed inside the final quotation mark.

Examples:

> "The bus is here," she said.
>
> She said, "The bus is here."

A semicolon or colon is <u>always outside</u> the quotation marks.

Examples:

> One computer shop owner said, "The program will cost $295"; another told me he would sell it to me for $225.
>
> John itemized my basic computer start-up needs: "disk drives, screen, keyboard, and printer."

Proper placement of question marks and exclamation marks can present problems.

If the end mark is part of the quotation, place a question mark or exclamation mark inside the final quotation mark.

Examples:

> "Where are my shoes?" asked Tina.
>
> "You won the prize!" shouted Melvin.

Sometimes the question mark or exclamation mark refers to the entire sentence rather than just the quoted material. If so, the mark goes <u>outside</u> the quotation mark.

Example:

> Did I understand you to have said, "You sold the last ticket five minutes ago"?

Occasionally you will write a quoted sentence that needs an exclamation mark or a question mark while the rest of the sentence needs a period. When this happens, omit the period.

Example:

> His brother asked, "What time are we leaving?"

Special Situations

Special situations that require the use of quotation marks include: writing dialogues, quotations of more than one paragraph, and quotations within other directly quoted material.

Dialogue

From time to time, if you are a typical writer, you will find yourself writing dialogue. As you write dialogue, start a new paragraph each time you change speakers.

Example:

"You . . . seem like old friends."

"I suppose it depends on one's definition of the word friend," he answered.

Longer Quotations

Sometimes a quotation is longer than one paragraph. If so, put quotation marks at the beginning of each paragraph and at the end of the final paragraph.

In addition, you occasionally will have a quotation within a quotation. When you do, use single quotation marks to designate the quotation within a quotation.

Example:

Nathan said, "Mom said 'be home by 10 p.m.' when I told her I was leaving."

Italics and More Quotation Marks

Italics and quotation marks are used to set some titles, names, and words apart from the rest of the text in books and other printed material. Underlining is substituted for italics in handwritten or typed material. Since some of the more sophisticated printers will print in italics, use that feature if available. Rather than continually add the explanation, keep in mind throughout this section that when the word "italics" is used, you will underline the words if you don't have the printer capability to do italics.

Italics are used to emphasize titles of long written works and the titles of publications that are published as a single work.

Examples:

Titles of Books: *The Day Lincoln Was Shot* by Jim Bishop

Titles of Plays: *Our Town*

Titles of Periodicals: *Newsweek*

Titles of Newspapers: *The Topeka Capital-Journal*

Titles of Long Poems: *Iliad*

Note: Newspaper names sometimes cause problems as the portion to be in italics varies from paper to paper. For example, *The New York Times* should <u>always</u> be fully capitalized and in italics. On the other hand, some papers can be handled in one of two ways. For example, it can be: the *Los Angeles Times* or the Los Angeles *Times*.

If you do not know the actual name of the paper, pick one of these later two forms and use it consistently.

In addition, titles of movies, television and radio series, and works of music and art are italicized.

Artistic Works Titles That Are Italicized

Titles of Movies: *Moon Over Miami*

Titles of Radio & TV Series: *Laverne & Shirley*

Titles of Long Musical Compositions and Record Albums (any musical work made up of several parts, such as operas, musical comedies, symphonies, and ballets): *Carmen, An American in Paris, Swan Lake*

Titles of Paintings & Sculpture: *American Gothic, David*

Some names are in italics including the names of individual air, sea, space, and land craft.

Air: *Spruce Goose*

Sea: *Bismarck* (German Battleship)

Space: *Voyager IV*

Land: the *Thomas Flyer* (race car)

Note: If *the* precedes the name, do <u>not</u> put *the* in italics or capitalize it because *the* is not considered part of the official name. Also, a specific name given to a group of vehicles (for example, the Ford Mustangs) is capitalized but is *not* italicized.

When using foreign phrases, italicize any that retain their foreign spelling and pronunciation. Since words and phrases constantly are being incorporated into the English language, it is a good idea to check a current dictionary. If the word is in the dictionary and is labeled with the name of a foreign language italicize it. However, if no language label exists, consider it as an English word and <u>do not</u> italicize it. If the foreign word is not in the dictionary, consider it foreign and italicize it.

Some words, letters, or numbers need to be italicized when used as names for themselves.

Examples:

Words: Did you mean to use the word *their* or *there*?

Letters: Be sure to cross the letter *t* and dot the letter *i*.

Numbers: If you are not careful when writing numerals, you can confuse the numbers *one* and *seven*.

Still More Quotation Marks

Besides all their other jobs, quotation marks enclose the titles of short literary works. Traditionally the designation short works include short stories, chapters from books, one-act plays, short poems, essays, and articles.

Examples:

> **Short Stories:** "To Build a Fire" by Jack London
>
> **Chapter From a Book:** "Before You Begin"
>
> **One-Act Play:** "Comin' 'Round The Mountain" by Ned Albert
>
> **Short Poem:** "The Purist" by Ogden Nash
>
> **Essay Title:** "The Voyage" by Washington Irving
>
> **Article Title:** "The Wily Weed"

In addition, certain television titles, music, and art need quotation marks. Place quotation marks around the titles of episodes in a series, songs, and parts of a long musical composition.

> **TV Episode:** "Something Borrowed, Someone Blue" from *Murder, She Wrote.*
>
> **Song Title:** "With a Song in My Heart"
>
> **Part of a Long Musical Composition:** "The Blue Bird" from Act 3 of *Sleeping Beauty.*

Sometimes you may need to refer to a title of one long work contained in a longer work. Referred to individually, each title would be italicized. When they are used together, however, another rule is used.

When a title of a work is mentioned as part of a collection, use quotation marks around it.

Example:

> "Tale of Two Cities" from *Works of Charles Dickens*

Titles without Italics or Quotation Marks

Two groups of titles appear to need italics or quotation marks but do not use them. The first group consists of titles of various religious works. You do <u>not</u> italicize or place in quotation marks any mention of the Bible, its books, divisions, or versions, nor do you use italics when referring to holy scriptures of other religions, e.g., the Koran or the Book of Mormon.

Example:

He found the Bible verse he was looking for in Genesis.

In addition, do <u>not</u> use italics with, nor place in quotation marks, the titles of government charters, alliances, treaties, acts, statutes, or reports.

Examples:

Bill of Rights

Mayflower Compact

Dashes and Parentheses

Dashes, like commas and parentheses, separate certain words, phrases, and clauses from the rest of the sentence. As a writer, you need to acquaint yourself with the different qualities of each. Since the comma is the most frequently used, it draws the least attention to itself.

The dash sets off material more dramatically. It is much more eye-catching and creates an extra space between the main part of the sentence and the part it is setting off. It often is used to enclose editorial remarks by the writer. Parentheses tend to be more reserved. (How about that, we're personifying punctuation!) They also can set off technical or explanatory material from the rest of the sentence.

Your decisions about which marks to use will depend mostly on your purpose for writing.

Dash

The dash [—] is used to set off dramatic or sudden changes in a sentence.

Example:

> You won't believe what I just saw—but it's too horrible to even think about!

Use dashes to set off words or phrases that separate parts of the main sentence.

Example:

> Oat bran—which is being hailed as a major health breakthrough—is now found in ice cream.

Note: If the interrupting idea is written as an exclamation or a question, put the appropriate punctuation mark before the last dash.

Example:

> Thursday—have you heard a weather report for that day?— we are planning a golf outing.

A dash can set off a dramatic summary statement. Used this way, the dash points back to what has already been written; an explanation or summary in more detail follows the dash.

Example:

> To win the contest—that was his grandest aspiration.

Another use of dashes is to set off certain nonessential appositives. There are four situations when you can use dashes with nonessential appositives:

1. When the appositive is long: Our doctor—who considers himself the resident comedian—is always telling jokes.

2. When the appositive is already punctuated: The boys— Jason, and of course, Harry—are going fishing tomorrow.

3. When it is introduced by words such as for example or that is: Some books—for example, *The Ambassadors* by Henry James— can be difficult reading.

4. When you want to be especially striking: Those books—all on the best-seller list—do not interest me.

Sometimes you will want to use dashes to set off a *nonessential modifier*. You can set it off with dashes when the modifier is already punctuated or when you want to add special emphasis.

Examples:

    Internal punctuation: My boss—who, without any explanation, gave me a raise—now expects me to work overtime.

    Strong emphasis: The extra pay—as I am sure my boss thought it would—is decreasing my objections to working overtime.

Finally, we come to the last kind of sentence interrupter—a parenthetical expression. As you remember, a parenthetical expression consists of words or phrases inserted into a sentence that have no essential grammatical relationship to it.

Dashes are used to set off parenthetical expressions when:

    1. The expression is long.

    2. It is already punctuated.

    3. You want to be especially dramatic.

Example:

> At their 60th wedding anniversary party—very few couples are married that long—more than two hundred guests wished them well.

Note: You will not use dashes with all parenthetical expressions. For example, if the expression is quite short, it would look silly with dashes.

Example:

Incorrect: They will—I suppose—be late again.

Correct: They will, I suppose, be late again.

A word of warning: Don't overuse dashes. Using an occasional dash can add variety and interest to your writing. Too many will cause them to lose their intended effect and may annoy your readers.

Parentheses

Although parentheses do not possess the showiness of the dash, they are the strongest separator you can use.

One use is to set off asides and explanations that are not essential to the meaning of the sentence. Read the sentence without the information to be sure it is not essential before putting it in parentheses.

Example:

> The packets of necessary materials (information brochure, city map, notebook, and pencil) are on the table in the lobby.

Sometimes asides and explanations may consist of one or more complete sentences. Parentheses can set off these longer interruptions too.

Example:

> The store will deliver my new computer tomorrow. (The owner said he would deliver it personally.) By tomorrow evening, I will be using some of my new programs.

Parentheses can set off supplementary numbers. They also can set off the dates of a person's birth and death or other nations that involve numbers.

Example:

> The class is studying several stories written by Mark Twain (1835-1910), and will read "The Notorious Jumping Frog of Calaveras County" next week. All the members (45) present voted "yes."

In addition, you should illustrate in parentheses any numbers you fear may be misread.

Example:

> It will take at least one thousand dollars ($1,000) to upgrade my computer.
>
> When using numbers or letters to mark items in a series, use parentheses around them to avoid confusion.

Example:

> The next time you get gas have the attendant check the: (1) oil; (2) air in tires (3) air filter; and (4) transmission fluid.
>
> Who was the first conspirator to stab Julius Caesar? (a) Casca (b) Brutus (c) Cassius

While you can use the parentheses in the following four ways, be careful not to overwork them:

1. Do <u>not</u> capitalize the initial word or use any end marks within the parentheses when a parenthetical phrase or declarative sentence interrupts another sentence.

Example:

> Tacos (my brother ate them for the first time in Los Angeles) are now his favorite Mexican food.

2. Use both an initial capital and an end mark inside the parentheses when a parenthetical question or exclamatory sentence interrupts another sentence.

Example:

> *Major Dad* (Isn't that a funny program?) is my favorite television sitcom.

3. If a parenthetical sentence comes between two complete sentences, use both an initial capital letter and an end mark inside the parentheses.

Example:

> I flew to Los Angeles to visit my cousin. (The flight from Kansas City took four hours.) I saw many historic sights while I was there.

4. Remember, punctuation that belongs to the main sentence usually will follow a parenthetical phrase. Any punctuation (commas, semicolons, colons, and end marks) belonging to the main sentence that follows a parenthetical phrase goes outside and after the second parentheses.

Example:

> It was cold for May (32° to be exact), and I had left my coat at home.

Hyphens

A hyphen is a multi-purpose form of punctuation. It can divide some numbers and parts of words; it can join compound words; it can divide words at the ends of lines.

With Numbers

A hyphen is used when writing out numbers from twenty-one through ninety-nine.

Examples:

forty-four   sixty-seven   eighty-nine

In addition, use a hyphen when writing a fraction as an adjective.

Example:

A two-thirds vote is needed for approval.

However, when the fraction is used as a noun, the hyphen is omitted.

Example:

One fourth of the students have had the measles.

With Word Parts

When a prefix is followed by a proper noun or a proper adjective, use a hyphen between them.

Examples:

mid-July   post-Civil War

In addition, some prefixes and suffixes require a hyphen even when there is no proper noun or proper adjective. The prefixes *all-*, *ex-*, *self-*, and the suffix *-elect* all use a hyphen.

Examples:

all-knowing; ex-congressman; self-important; governor-elect

Note: Be sure that a complete word joins the prefix or suffix. When the prefix or suffix is part of the main word, do not use a hyphen.

Example:

Incorrect: ex-ecutor
Correct: executor

With Compound Words

Unless the dictionary gives a different spelling, use a hyphen to join two or more words that are used as one word.

Example:

mother-in-law

Since hyphen use in compound words is always changing, it is a good idea to check your dictionary before inserting or dropping a hyphen.

When a compound modifier comes before a noun, use a hyphen to connect its parts.

Example:

The well-groomed applicant got the job.

However, when the compound modifier follows the noun, the hyphen is not used.

Example:

The applicant, who was well groomed, got the job.

Exception: If a compound modifier is hyphenated in the dictionary it will retain the hyphen regardless of its position in the sentence.

Hyphens are <u>not</u> used with a compound modifier that includes a word ending in -*ly* or in a compound proper adjective or a compound proper noun acting as an adjective.

Example:

> **Incorrect:** The beautifully-embroidered tapestry had been imported from India.
>
> **Correct:** The beautifully embroidered tapestry had been imported from India.

For Clarity

When a particular combination of letters could be confusing to the reader, use a hyphen within the word to avoid confusion.

Example:

> re-formed — reformed
>
> re-lay — relay

In addition, unusual combinations of words can be clarified with hyphens. The hyphen will help the reader understand which words belong together.

Example:

> a new home-owner — a new-home owner
>
> twenty five-cent stamps — twenty-five cent stamps
>
> back-up disks — back up the disks

Hyphens at Ends of Lines

Decisions. Decisions. That's what you have when you come to the end of a line of writing. If you use a typewriter, you can release the right margin and sneak a few extra letters in. Word processing programs (at least the ones I'm familiar with) won't let you do that. But which looks best? Is it better to sneak those few extra letters in, drop the word to the next line, or divide the word? If you decide to divide it, you will use a hyphen and follow these rules of proper hyphen use.

1. Any division that is done must be done between syllables. If in doubt where a syllable break occurs, check the dictionary.

2. Do <u>not</u> divide one syllable words. Most of these are easy to spot, but some one syllable words, for example *through,* sound like they have two syllables. If in doubt, check it out.

3. Do <u>not</u> divide a word leaving a single letter by itself on a line.

4. Do not divide proper nouns and adjectives.

5. If you have to divide a word that already has a hyphen in it, the division is made at the hyphen.

6. <u>Never</u> divide a word at the end of a page so that part of it is on one page and the rest on the next one. In fact, some publishers do not even want words divided at the ends of lines. However, you would need to check the guidelines of each publication on that.

Apostrophes

The last punctuation mark we will consider is the apostrophe. With the possible exception of the comma, the apostrophe is more misused and abused than any other punctuation mark. Since its misuse can cause words to be misspelled and can change their meanings, be sure to use it properly.

Some people seem to think that every time they encounter an -*s* at the end of a word they should put an apostrophe with it. Not true. The two jobs of the apostrophe are to show possession and to indicate missing letters.

With Possessive Nouns

Indicate possession (ownership) with nouns by using an apostrophe.

With Singular Nouns

To show the possessive case of <u>most</u> singular nouns, add an apostrophe and -*s*.

Examples:

> books of the student — student's books
>
> wishes of the client — client's wishes
>
> hem of the dress — dress's hem

Note: Most of the time you will add an -'*s* (as in the last example) even when the singular noun ends in -*s*. However, if the additional -s makes the word difficult to pronounce leave it off.

With Plural Nouns

To show the possessive case of plural nouns ending in -*s* or -*es*, add an apostrophe after the -*s*.

Examples:

> difficulty of the cases — cases' difficulty
>
> voices of the singers — singers' voices

When the plural noun does not end in -*s* or -*es*, add an apostrophe and -*s* to show the possessive case.

Examples:

> purses of the women — women's purses
>
> horns of the cattle — cattle's horns

With Compound Nouns

Sometimes the noun showing ownership consists of more than one word. In these cases the apostrophe and -*s* or just an apostrophe if the word is a plural form ending in -*s* is added to the last word in the compound noun.

Examples:

sister-in-law's book

editor-in-chief's desk

Time, Amount and Word <u>Sake</u>

Use an apostrophe and -*s* or just an apostrophe, (depending on whether the possessive is singular or plural) when forming possessives involving time, amounts, or the word *sake*.

Examples:

Time: a week's travel, three years' time

Amount: dime's worth, seventy-five cents' worth

Sake: for goodness' sake

Ownership

When two nouns precede a possession, accurate placement of the apostrophe is vital. If misplaced, the appositive can give inaccurate information about the ownership.

If you want to show joint ownership (they own the possession together) add an apostrophe and -*s* to the last noun in a series.

Example:

George and Melissa's car is in the repair shop.

If you want to show individual ownership (they each own a separate possession), add an apostrophe and -*s* at the end of each noun in a series.

Example:

> George's and Melissa's cars are in the repair shop.

With Pronouns

<u>Some</u> pronouns that show ownership require an apostrophe. An apostrophe and -*s* are used with indefinite pronouns to show possession.

Examples:

> anyone's
> nobody's
> another's

However, you do <u>not use an apostrophe with the possessive forms of personal pronouns</u>. *His, hers, theirs, its, ours, your, yours,* and *whose* already show ownership.

Note: Be careful when using the pronouns whose and its as they sometimes are confused with the contractions *who's* and *it's*.

With Contractions

An apostrophe is used with contractions to show the position of the missing letter or letters. It is quite common for verbs to be used in a contracted form.

Examples:

> I'll (I will); can't (cannot); he'll (he will)

Note: *Will not* **becomes** *won't* when used as a contraction.

Contractions should not be used in formal writing. You will have to determine how formal you want your writing to be and gauge your use of contractions accordingly.

Example:

Informal: She's promised to take us to a movie if we'll study hard for the test.

Formal: She has promised to take us to a movie if we will study hard for the test.

With Years

If a number or numbers are left out when writing a year, insert an apostrophe in place of the missing numbers.

Example:

graduating class of '92

Contractions with o', d', and l'

These letters followed by the apostrophe create the abbreviated form of the words *of the* or *the* as spelled in various languages.

Examples:

o'clock, O'Malley

With Dialogue

You often use contractions when writing dialogue as most people speak more informally than they write. In addition, if you are writing dialogue to include a regional dialect or a foreign accent, you will often use apostrophes to indicate unusual pronunciations or omitted letters.

Example:

Y' all come, y' hear?

A word of caution: Be judicious in your use of dialect as it can make reading difficult and slow down the flow. It will annoy your readers if they have to decipher what a character is saying. Use just enough dialect to give the desired flavor without bogging your writing down.

Special Uses

When writing the plurals of numbers, symbols, letters, and words used to name themselves, use an apostrophe and -*s*.

Examples:

> 75's (if written in words, it does not need an apostrophe)
>
> 4 ?'s
>
> trouble distinguishing between *g's* and *q's*
>
> *four's* and *for's* cause confusion

Conclusion

If you practice the style rules you have reviewed in this chapter, your writing should be clearer and more understandable. That will make for happy editors and readers.

Chapter 16:

Grammar Definitions

Abbreviate: to shorten an existing word or phrase.

Action verb: a verb that tells what action someone or something is performing. It may be transitive or intransitive depending on whether or not it transfers its action to another word in the sentence.

Active verb: its subject performs the action.

Adjective: a word used to describe a noun or pronoun or to give a noun or pronoun a more specific meaning. It answers any of these four questions: what kind? which one? how many? or how much?

Adjectival phrase: a prepositional phrase that modifies a noun or pronoun by telling what kind or which one.

Adverbial phrase: a prepositional phrase that modifies a verb, adjective, or adverb by pointing out where, when, in what manner, or to what extent.

Adverb: a word that modifies a verb, an adjective, or another adverb. When modifying a verb it answers one of the following questions: where? when? in what manner? to what extent?

Antecedent: the noun, or group of words acting as a noun, for which a pronoun stands.

Appositive: a noun or pronoun placed after another noun or pronoun to identify, rename, or explain it.

Appositive phrase: a noun or pronoun with modifiers, placed next to a noun or pronoun to add information and details.

Capitalize: to begin a word with a capital letter.

Case: the form of a noun or pronoun that indicates how it is used in a sentence.

Clause: a group of words that has its own subject and verb.

Common noun: any one of a class of people, places, things, or ideas.

Complement: a word or group of words that completes the meaning of the predicate of a sentence.

Compound adjective: an adjective that is made up of more than one word: freeze-dried; nearsighted.

Compound noun: a noun that is made up of more than one word.

Compound subject: two or more subjects that have the same verb and are joined by a conjunction such as *and* or *or*.

Compound verb: two or more verbs that have the same subject and are joined by a conjunction such as *and* or *or*.

Conjunction: a word used to connect other words or groups of words (e.g. and, but, both . . . and, neither . . . nor).

Conjunctive adverb: an adverb that acts as a conjunction to connect complete ideas.

Dangling modifier: seems to modify either the wrong word or no word at all because the word it should modify is missing from the sentence.

Declarative sentence: states an idea and ends with a period.

Demonstrative pronoun: a pronoun that directs attention to a specific person, place, thing, or idea.

Direct object: a noun, pronoun, or group of words acting as a noun that receives the action of a transitive verb.

Exclamatory sentence: conveys strong emotion and ends with an exclamation mark.

Fragment: a group of words that does not express a complete thought.

Helping verbs: verbs that can be added to another verb to make a single verb phrase.

Imperative sentence: gives an order or a direction and ends with a period or an exclamation mark.

Independent clause: can stand by itself as a complete sentence.

Indirect object: a noun or pronoun that comes after an action verb and before a direct object. Its purpose is to name the person or thing that something is given to or done for. Example: I threw John the ball.

Interjection: a word that expresses feeling or emotion and functions independently of a sentence.

Interrogative sentence: asks a question and ends with a question mark.

Intransitive verb: does not direct action toward someone or something named in the same sentence. Example: Jane lay down for a nap.

Linking verb: a verb that connects its subject with a word at or near the end of the sentence.

Misplaced modifier: seems to modify the wrong word in a sentence.

Modifier: Adjectives and adverbs are the two kinds of modifiers. They give additional information about nouns, pronouns, verbs, and other adjectives and adverbs. They should be placed as close as possible to the words they modify.

Nominative case pronoun: pronoun used as the subject of a verb and for a predicate nominate.

Noun: names a person, place, thing or idea.

Objective case pronoun: pronoun used as the object of any verb, verbal, or preposition.

Objective complement: an adjective, noun, or group of words acting as a noun that follow a direct object and describes or renames it.

Parallelism: the placement of equal ideas in words, phrases or clauses of similar types.

Participle: a form of a verb that acts as an adjective.

Participle phrase: a present or past participle that is modified by an adverb or adverbial phrase or that has a complement. The entire phrase acts as an adjective in a sentence.

Passive verb: always has a verb phrase containing a form of be and the past participle of a transitive verb. Its action is performed upon the subject.

Phrase: a group of words, without a subject and verb, that functions in a sentence as one part of speech, e.g., prepositional phrases, appositive phrases, gerund phrases, and infinitive phrases.

Predicate adjective: an adjective that follows a linking verb and describes the subject of the sentence.

Predicate nominative: a noun or pronoun that follows a linking verb and renames, identifies, or explains the subject of the sentence.

Preposition: a word that relates the noun or pronoun following it to another word in the sentence.

Pronoun: a word used to take the place of a noun or group of words acting as a noun.

Proper adjective: an adjective formed from a proper noun: Shakespeare— Shakespearean.

Proper noun: names a specific person, place, thing, or idea.

Relative pronoun: a pronoun that begins a subordinate clause and relates it to another idea in the sentence.

Run-on sentence: two or more complete sentences that are capitalized and punctuated as if they were one.

Sentence: a group of words with two main parts. It contains a complete subject and a complete predicate. Together they express a complete thought.

Simple predicate: the essential verb or verb phrase that cannot be left out of the complete predicate.

Simple subject: the essential noun, pronoun, or group of words acting as a noun that cannot be left out of the complete subject.

Subject complement: a noun, pronoun, or adjective that follows a linking verb and tells something about the subject of the sentence.

Subordinate clause: although it has a subject and verb, cannot stand by itself as a complete sentence; it can only be part of a sentence.

Tense: a form of a verb that shows time of action or state of being.

Transitive verb: directs action toward someone or something named in the same sentence. Example: He hit the ball. Ball received the action *hit.*

Verb: a word that expresses time while showing an action, a condition, or the fact that something exists. A verb has four principal parts: the present, the present participle, the past, and the past participle.

Voice: the form a verb takes to show whether or not the subject is performing the action.

Bibliography

Albert, F.S.C., Brother H., et al. *English Arts and Skills, Grade 11*. The Macmillan Company. New York, New York. 1966.

Allen, Walter, (edited by). *Writers on Writing*. The Writer, Inc. Boston, Massachusetts. 1988.

Bates, Jefferson D. *Writing With Precision*. Acropolis

Books Ltd. Washington, D.C. 1980.

Berbrich, Joan D. *Writing Creatively*. Amsco School Publications, Inc. New York, New York. 1977.

Brown, Ann Cole, Jeffery Nilson, Fran Weber Shaw, Richard A. Weldon. *Grammar and Composition, Fifth Course*. Houghton Mifflin Company. Boston, Massachusetts. 1984.

Burack, Sylvia K. (Edited by). *The Writer's Handbook*. The Writer, Inc. Boston, Massachusetts. 1990.

Card, Orson Scott. *Characters & Viewpoint*. Writer's Digest Books. Cincinnati, Ohio. 1988.

Cool, Lisa Collier. *How to Sell Every Magazine Article You Write*. Writer's Digest Books Cincinnati, Ohio. 1986.

Dibell, Ansen. *Plot.* Writer's Digest Books. Cincinnati, Ohio. 1988.

Editorial Staff of the University of Chicago Press. *The Chicago Manual of Style*. The University of Chicago Press. Chicago, Illinois. 1982.

Farlini, Gary (prepared by). *Grammar and Composition, Level 4*. Prentice-Hall, Inc. Englewood Cliffs, New Jersey. 1982.

Fowler, H. Ramsey. *The Little Brown Handbook, Second Edition*. Little, Brown and Company. Boston, Massachusetts. 1983.

Glatthorn, Allan A., et al. *The English Book 4 A Complete Course*. Science Research Associates, Inc. Chicago, Illinois. 1981.

Guth, Hans P. *Words and Ideas, Second Edition*. Wadsworth Publishing Company, Inc. Belmont, California. 1966.

Hensley, Dennis E. *Writing For Profit*. Thomas Nelson Publishers. Nashville, Tennessee. 1985.

Leggett, Glenn C., David Mead, William Charvat. *Handbook For Writers, Sixth Edition*. Prentice-Hall, Inc. Englewood Cliffs, New Jersey. 1974.

Lutz, William. *Doublespeak*. Harper & Row, Publishers. New York, New York. 1989.

Macrorie, Ken. *Telling Writing*. Hayden Book Company, Inc. New York, New York. 1970.

McCrimmon, James M. *Writing With A Purpose, Fifth Edition.* Houghton Mifflin Company. Boston, Massachusetts. 1972.

Murray, Donald M. *A Writer Teaches Writing: A Practical Method of Teaching Composition.* Houghton Mifflin Company. Boston, Massachusetts. 1968.

Newcomb, Duane. *How to Sell & Re-sell Your Writing.* Writer's Digest Books. Cincinnati, Ohio. 1987.

Owen, Jean Z. *Professional Fiction Writing.* The Writer, Inc. Boston, Massachusetts. 1978.

Polking, Kirk, Joan Bloss, Colleen Cannon. *Writer's Encyclopedia.* Writer's Digest Books. Cincinnati, Ohio. 1983.

Stegner, Dr. Wallace E., Dr. Edwin H. Sauer, Mr. Clarence W. Hach, Mrs. Jane Rummel. *Modern Composition, Book 1.* Holt, Rinehart and Winston, Inc. 1965.

Stegner, Dr. Wallace E., Dr. Edwin H. Sauer, Mr. Clarence W. Hach, Mrs. Jane Rummel. *Modern Composition, Book 2.* Holt, Rinehart and Winston, Inc. 1965.

Vivante, Arturo. *Writing Fiction.* The Writer, Inc. Boston, Massachusetts. 1980.

Walker, Robert. *Leads and Story Openings.* Creation House. Carol Stream, Illinois. 1985.

Warriner, John E. *English Grammar and Composition, Third Course.* Harcourt Brace Jovanovich, Publishers. New York, New York. 1982.

Young, Woody. *A Business Guide to © Copyright Law: What You Don't Know Can Co$t You!*. Joy Publishing. San Juan Capistrano, California. 1988.

Index

About the Author

LOMA G. DAVIES has a master's degree from Purdue University - Calumet, Hammond, Indiana. She taught high school for seventeen years in Hobart, Indiana, ten years of which she taught English, creative writing and composition classes. She is presently an instructor of freshman English for Highland Junior College, Highland, Kansas.

Several of her more than 300 published articles deal with topics covered in this book. She has freelanced for more than forty magazines, including *Field and Stream* and *Saturday Evening Post*. In addition, she is the staff writer for SAKW (State Association of Kansas Watersheds) and is a correspondent and weekly columnist for the Topeka Capital-Journal and the Wamego Smoke Signal. She is author of the book *201 Happy Hints*.

Since 1988 she has spoken at several writing conferences, including the Lamplighters in Newton, Kansas; Christian Writers Institute in Wheaton, Illinois; the Write-To-Publish Conference at Moody Bible Institute in Chicago; and the Florida State Writers Conference. In addition, she is a member of the Topeka Writers Group and does the instructional section of each meeting. She also teaches individual students and gives talks on creative writing at area schools.

☆ Share The Success Secrets of
66 Established Freelance Writers

Order your copy of
Writers At Work
today!

Find out:

- ➡ *How to collect on past-due accounts*
- ➡ *How to beat writer's block*
- ➡ *How to schedule multiple tasks*
- ➡ *How to find time to write*
- ➡ *How to set up an office area*
- ➡ *How to work in and around your family*
- ➡ *... and much, much more*

This book is an indispensable tool for success. Discover how other writers are meeting the same challenges you face.

Having trouble writing around kids, spouses and other jobs? Read how other successful writers do it.

Become more *successful* ... and make your writing even more *profitable*.

$ $ Increase Your Income & Beat Writer's Block $ $

Got a Minute?

101
Marketing Tips for Writers

by Rebecca Rohan

This book will teach you the valuable money making methods, quick tips and new ideas that you need to market your writing skills most effectively.

Read each tip in less than a minute!

You'll discover:

- *How to market more efficiently using "editor files"*
- *Additional markets that are probably already in your office...but you're not using*
- *Four ways to market interviewing skills*
- *Three tips for coming up with that "Big Idea"*
- *How to request guidelines and sample copies*
- *A new way of digging out markets*
- *How to "process" writer guidelines*
- *A "different" market for fantasy / adventure*
- *How to make money in Technical Writing, Mystery Parties, Proofreading, etc.*
- *How to make money with fax machines*
- *...and much, much more*